Land Law

Fifth Edition

Routledge·Cavendish
Taylor & Francis Group
ROUTLEDGE

Fifth edition published 2007
by Routledge•Cavendish
2 Park Square, Milton Park, Abingdon, Oxon, OX14 4RN

Simultaneously published in the USA and Canada
by Routledge•Cavendish
270 Madison Ave, New York, NY 10016

*Routledge•Cavendish is an imprint of the Taylor & Francis Group,
an informa business*

© 2007 Routledge•Cavendish

First edition published by Cavendish Publishing 1996
Second edition published by Cavendish Publishing 1999
Third edition published by Cavendish Publishing 2002
Fourth edition published by Cavendish Publishing 2004

Typeset in Helvetica by Florence Production Ltd, Stoodleigh, Devon
Printed and bound in the UK by Ashford Colour Press, Gosport

Library of Congress Cataloging in Publication Data
A catalog record for this book has been requested

ISBN10: 1–84568–016–2

ISBN13: 978–1–84568–016–9

Contents

Abbreviations

Titles of Acts and Rules used repeatedly in the text are abbreviated as follows. (Their dates are given in the text.)

AEA	Administration of Estates Act
AJA	Administration of Justice Act
CAA	Civil Aviation Act
CPR	Civil Procedure Rules
C(ROTP)A	Contacts (Rights Of Third Parties) Act
HA	Housing Act
LA	Limitation Act
LCA	Land Charges Act
LPA	Law of Property Act
LP(MP)A	Law of Property (Miscellaneous Provisions) Act
LRA	Land Registration Act
LRR	Land Registration Rules
LTA	Landlord and Tenant Act
LT(C)A	Landlord and Tenant (Covenants) Act
PEA	Protection from Eviction Act
RA	Rent Act
SLA	Settled Land Act
TA	Trustee Act
TCPA	Town and Country Planning Act
TOLATA	Trusts of Land and Appointment of Trustees Act
WA	Wills Act

1 Fundamental concepts

Statutory definitions of land

- '"Land" includes land of any tenure and mines and minerals, whether or not held apart from the surface, buildings or parts of buildings . . . and other corporeal hereditaments; also a manor, an advowson, and a rent and other corporeal hereditaments, and an easement, right, privilege, or benefit in, over, or derived from land . . .': s 205(1)(ix) of the LPA 1925, amended by Sched 4 to the TOLATA 1996.

- '"Land" includes buildings and other structures, land covered with water, and any estate, interest, easement, servitude or right in or over land': Sched 1 to the Interpretation Act 1978.

- 'Land includes–
  (a) buildings and other structures,
  (b) land covered with water, and
  (c) mines and minerals, whether or not held with the surface.'
  (Section 132(1) of the LRA 2002.)

- 'Hereditament' refers to real property capable of being inherited.

- Traditionally, ownership of land has been held to be ownership of a space from the highest heavens down to the centre of the earth, but this view has been modified by the requirements of modern life (see, for example, the CAA 1982; Treasure Act 1996; *Wollerton and Wilson Ltd v Richard Costain Ltd* (1970) – liability for overhanging crane jib; *Bernstein v Skyviews and General Ltd* (1978) – no liability in trespass for aircraft flying over land at a reasonable height; *Laiqat v Majid* (2005) – liability for extraction duct which encroached onto neighbouring land by 750mm).

Concept of property

Problems of property arising where chattels are affixed to land

Problems may emerge from interpretation of the old maxim: 'Whatever is annexed to the soil becomes a part thereof.' Section 62(1) of the LPA 1925 tells us that all fixtures are conveyed with the land, unless there is a contrary intention expressed in the conveyance (s 62(4)). How do we decide whether or not an item is a fixture? (See figure on page 4.)

There are two tests to help us decide whether or not a chattel has been annexed to (become part of) the land

Degree of annexation test. This test operates by way of presumption – the more firmly a chattel is attached to the land, the more likely it is to be a fixture (*Holland v Hodgson* (1872) – looms bolted to stone floors were fixtures). An important question is whether significant damage would be caused by removal of the chattel (*Elitestone v Morris* (1997) – bungalow resting on concrete pillars)

Object (or purpose) of annexation test. The chattel will be a fixture if it was placed on the land with the intention of improving the realty The effect of this test may be to rebut the presumption raised by the degree of annexation test. Firmly attached chattels (eg, television aerials) may be chattels, whereas chattels resting on their own weight may be fixtures if they contribute to the overall architectural design (*D'Eyncourt v Gregory* (1886) – garden seats and vases held to be fixtures)

Fixtures may be removed lawfully from land in the cases of:

- *Mortgagor and mortgagee* – where land has been mortgaged, fixtures may be included in the mortgage. (*TSB Bank v Botham* (1996)).

- *Landlord and tenant* – in general, the landlord is entitled to fixtures attached by the tenant. There are exceptions in cases of agricultural fixtures, trade fixtures (which may be removed before but not after the end of tenancy) and ornamental fixtures (which can be removed without causing substantial injury to property).

  There is a common law duty to make good any damage caused by removal of tenants' fixtures and to leave the premises in reasonable condition. Liability at common law is on the person who removed the fixtures (*Mancetter Developments v Garmanson* (1986)).

- *Vendor and purchaser* – under a conveyance, fixtures pass to a purchaser without express mention (s 62(1) of the LPA 1925), unless there is a contrary intention expressed in the conveyance (s 62(4)).

Concept of tenure and estates

Tenure is concerned with the conditions upon which land is held. It answers the question: *how* is land held? Today, all land is held by the Crown, directly or indirectly. *Estate* is concerned with the length of time for which a tenant may hold land. It answers the question: for *how long* is land held?

Concepts of rights, estates and interests

Generally speaking, when you hold an estate in the land you have 'ownership' of the land. If you have an interest in land you have an interest (for example, a right of way) in or over land owned by somebody else.

Legal rights are rights *in rem*, binding 'the entire world'. *Equitable rights* are rights *in personam*, binding all persons other than the *bona fide* purchaser of a legal estate without notice of such (equitable) rights.

Section 1 of the LPA 1925

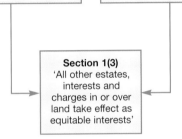

Section 1(1)
Only two legal estates:
fee simple absolute in
possession – freehold – lasts
virtually for ever;
term of years absolute –
leasehold – lasts for some
determinate period (a week, a
month, a thousand years, etc)

Section 1(2)
*Only five interests which may
be legal* (ie, these interests
may be legal or equitable):
easement; rentcharge; charge
by way of legal mortgage; any
other similar charge created
by instrument; rights of entry
exercisable over a legal lease
or rentcharge

Section 1(3)
'All other estates,
interests and
charges in or over
land take effect as
equitable interests'

Concept of 'purchaser without notice'

An equitable interest may be enforced against all persons,
except a *bona fide* purchaser, for value of the legal estate who
has taken without notice of the existence of that interest, and
against one who claims through him:

- *'Bona fide'* – the purchaser must have acted in good faith
  and without fraud.

- *'Purchaser'* – one who takes property by sale or gift, and not
  merely by operation of law (as on an intestacy). Includes
  mortgagee and lessee.

- *'Value'* – refers to any consideration in money, money's worth, or consideration of a future marriage (*Salih v Atchi* (1961)). Should the purchaser acquire a legal estate and not give value, he will take subject to all existing equitable rights.

- *'Legal estate'* – this refers to legal fee simple absolute or legal term of years.

- *'Without notice'* – a purchaser with notice of the equitable interest will usually take the estate subject to that interest.

Concept of 'notice'

'Notice' refers to awareness of some event or state of affairs. It does not include giving one's attention to vague rumours (*Barnhart v Greenshields* (1853)). The doctrine of notice applies only to land with unregistered title. 'The law as to notice . . . has no application even by analogy to registered land' (*Williams & Glyn's Bank v Boland* (1981), *per* Lord Wilberforce).

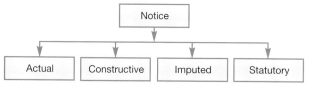

- *Actual notice* – the purchaser is made expressly aware during negotiations of some prior equitable interest. Since 1926, actual notice has only applied to residual interests in unregistered land. A residual equitable interest is one that is neither overreachable nor capable of entry in the Land Charges Register.

- *Constructive notice* – the purchaser is deemed to have been given such notice if he could have discovered the interest had he made the appropriate inquiries, for example, by inspecting the land (see *Hunt v Luck* (1902) – purchaser fixed with constructive notice of the rights of those in occupation of the land); s 199 of the LPA 1925. Such notice may be presumed where there has been express notice of a fact which ought to have led to notice of other facts (*see Midland Bank v Farmpride Hatcheries* (1981)). Constructive notice applies only to residual interests in unregistered land.

- *Imputed notice* – the purchaser employs a solicitor or other agent, and their notice of claims is imputed to the purchaser (*Kingsnorth Finance Co Ltd v Tizard* (1986)). Imputed notice also only applies to residual interests in unregistered land.

- *Statutory notice* – statutory notice applies only to those interests in unregistered land which are capable of entry in the Land Charges Register. Section 198 of the LPA 1925 provides that registration of an interest in the Land Charges Register constitutes actual notice to all persons and for all purposes.

Concept of the fee simple absolute in possession

The largest estate known to English land law involves unlimited duration in time, with extensive powers over the land. It is known also as 'freehold estate':

- '*Fee*' denotes estate of inheritance, that is, it will not necessarily end on death of the owner. It will end only on failure of an appropriate successor in title.

- '*Simple*' denotes an ordinary fee capable of passing to general heirs and which carries no condition as to passing to one particular class of heir.

- '*Absolute*' denotes that the estate is not limited in time. A fee simple may not be absolute, for example, it is possible to create a determinable fee (one which will never determine unless something happens – eg, a fee simple until the United Kingdom leaves the European Union), or a conditional fee (one which will last for as long as a condition is complied with – eg, a fee to X and his heirs for as long as they reside in the property).

- '*In possession*' denotes an estate which is immediate, and, therefore, neither in reversion nor remainder. The phrase bestows 'a present right of present enjoyment' (see *Pearson v IRC* (1981)). It includes receipt of rents, profits, and the right to receive same: s 205(1)(xix) of the LPA 1925. ('Reversion': rights retained by grantor; 'remainder' – present right to some future enjoyment of land.)

Creation and transfer of estates and interests in land

Requirements for a valid contract for sale

Section 40 of the LPA 1925	Section 2 of the LP(MP)A 1989
Contracts before 27 September 1989	Contracts after 26 September 1989
Evidenced in writing	Contract in writing
	Containing all terms expressly agreed
Signed by the vendor or his agent	Signed by all parties
Exception: oral contract evidenced by act or part performance	Exceptions: resulting, implied or constructive trusts (s 2(5)); estoppel? – see *Yaxley v Gotts* (2000) and *Banner v Luff* developments (2000)
Otherwise, contract unenforceable	Otherwise, contract void

Requirements for a valid conveyance of land

All conveyances must be by deed (see s 52(1) of the LPA 1925).

Before 31 July 1990, deeds must be:	After 30 July 1990, deeds must be:
● signed; ● sealed; ● delivered.	● signed; ● delivered; ● witnessed; ● see s 1 of the LP(MP)A 1989; ● *Exception*: estoppel (see *Shah v Shah* (2001)).

2 Conveying title to land with unregistered title

Almost 20% of the land in England and Wales remains unregistered. The law concerning unregistered conveyancing is to be found in the common law, as modified by such statutes as the LPA 1925, the LPA 1969 and the LCA 1972.

(V = vendor; P = purchaser)

V's title is investigated by P's solicitor for existence of good root of title, which should be at least 15 years old (s 23 of the LPA 1969)
Epitome of V's chain of title is prepared
V's capacity to sell the property is checked
P makes survey of the property and his solicitor searches the Land Charges Register and the Register of Local Land Charges, etc
Draft contract is prepared by V's solicitor (s 2 of the LP(MP)A 1989). The draft contract is then sent to P's solicitor for approval
Contracts are exchanged
Delivery of the deed is effectively completion of transfer of land process
Stamp Duty Land Tax may be payable on the conveyance. Title to the land must also be registered at the Land Registry because all land in England and Wales is now subject to compulsory registration on sale (SI 1989/1347)

Will a purchaser be bound by interests in unregistered land?

 Legal rights, being rights *in rem*, will bind a purchaser.

 Equitable rights are of three types:

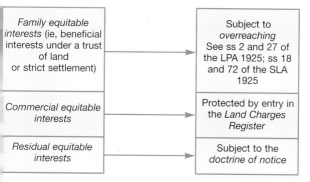

Overreaching beneficial interests in unregistered land

Beneficial interests under a trust of land or strict settlement will be swept off the land and into the purchase money provided that:

• In the case of a trust of land, a receipt for capital money is obtained from the trustees of land, being at least two in number or a trust corporation. A sole personal representative may also give a valid receipt.

• In the case of a strict settlement, the capital money is paid to the trustees, being at least two in number, or a trust corporation, or into court.

Registration of land charges

The system of registering land charges was introduced by the LCA 1925 (now LCA 1972). The system enables those who hold certain categories of interest in unregistered land to register the encumbrance in order to protect it against future purchasers of the land. The doctrine of notice no longer applies to these interests.

Registers under the LCA 1972 (kept by Registrar at Land Charges Department of Land Registry)

Register of Pending Actions

Includes actions or proceedings pending in court, relating to land or any interest in or charge on land, and petitions in bankruptcy.

Register of Annuities

No further entries are to be made in this register.

Register of Writs and Orders Affecting Land

Includes writs or orders affecting land issued to enforce a judgment or recognisance, bankruptcy orders, access orders under Access to Neighbouring Land Act 1992.

Register of Deeds of Arrangement

Involves documents under which the debtor makes arrangements in favour of creditors: see Deeds of Arrangement Act 1914; s 7 (1) of the LCA 1972.

Register of Land Charges

See below.

The six categories of land charge

Class A	LCA 1972, s 2 (2)	Rents or annuities not created by deed
Class B	LCA 1972, s 2 (3)	Land charges arising automatically by statute
Class C	LCA 1972, s 2 (4)	C(i) puisne mortgages: legal mortgages not protected by deposit of title deeds C(ii) limited owner's charges

		C(iii) general equitable charges C(iv) estate contracts: includes options to purchase and rights of pre-emption
Class D	LCA 1972, s 2 (5)	D(i) Inland Revenue charges D(ii) restrictive covenants created after 1925 D(iii) equitable easements created after 1925
Class E	LCA 1972, s 2 (6)	Annuities created before 1926 and not registered in the Register of Annuities
Class F	LCA 1972, s 2 (7)	Matrimonial home rights under the Family Law Act 1996. This provision enables a spouse who is not the legal owner of the land to register a right of occupation against the name of the legal owner

Features of the Land Charges Register

- Registration is made against the name of the estate owner. The correct name of the estate owner is deemed to be the name used in the conveyancing documents (*Standard Property Investments plc v British Plastics Federation* (1987)).

- Registration constitutes actual notice to all persons and for all purposes (s 198(1) of the LPA 1925).

- An official search certificate is conclusive (s 10(4) of the LCA 1972).

- Unregistered interests which fall into Classes A; B; C(i)–(iii); E; and F are void as against a purchaser of the land charged with it (s 4 of the LCA 1972).

- Unregistered interests which fall into Classes C(iv) and D will be void against a purchaser for money or money's worth (s 4(6) of the LCA 1972).

- A purchaser of the legal estate will take free from an unregistered interest even if he has actual knowledge of it. Notice and good faith are irrelevant. In the words of Lord Wilberforce, 'it is not "fraud" to rely on legal rights conferred by Act of Parliament' (*Midland Bank Trust Co v Green* (1981)).

Problems with the Land Charges Register

- Interests which are registered against the name of somebody who owned the land prior to the first conveyance older than 15 years. Such interests are binding even though they may be undiscoverable when the purchaser investigates the vendor's title (see s 23 of the LPA 1969).

- Misdescription of the land either by the person entering the interest or by the vendor when searching the register (see *Du Sautoy v Symes* (1967) and *Horrill v Cooper* (1998)).

- Registration or searching under the wrong name (see *Oak Co-operative Building Society v Blackburn* (1968) and *Diligent Finance Co v Alleyne* (1972)).

Register of Local Land Charges

- This has nothing to do with the Land Charges Register.

- Applies to both registered and unregistered land.

- Each district council or London borough keeps its own register of local land charges under the Local Land Charges Act 1975.

- The registers include such matters as planning applications and restrictions, and charges for the making up of a road, etc.

- Entries are registered against the address of the property and not against the landowner.

Residual interests

These interests remain subject to the doctrine of notice.

- Easements and restrictive covenants created before 1926.

- Equitable mortgages protected by deposit of title deeds.

- Beneficial interests under a trust when there is only one trustee (see *Kingsnorth Finance Co v Tizard* (1986)).

- Estoppel licences (see *Ives v High* (1967)).

- Rights acquired by the doctrine of mutual benefit and burden (see *Halsall v Brizell* (1957)).

- Equitable rights of entry (see *Shiloh Spinners v Harding* (1973)).

3 Transferring title to land with registered title

The law concerning land with registered title is to be found in the LRA 2002 and LRR 2003 (SI 2003/1417).

The conveyancing process is similar, but the following differences exist:

- Proof of title to the land is provided by registration at the Land Registry – not by deeds.
- The Land Charges Register and the doctrine of notice are irrelevant to registered land.
- The land is identified by a unique title number and incumbrances are registered against the title – not against the name of the legal proprietor.
- The vendor's solicitor no longer has to prepare an abstract or epitome of title – title is verified by official copies of register entries.
- A conveyance is now more correctly called a transfer.
- Legal title does not pass from vendor to purchaser with conveyance or transfer – the purchaser only becomes the legal proprietor when the disposition is registered at the Land Registry (s 27(1) of the LRA 2002).
- Registered conveyancing is likely to change considerably when the proposals for electronic conveyancing are fully implemented. See Pt 8 and Sched 5 to the LRA 2002.

Principles underlying registered land

Mirror principle

The rights and interests shown on the register should mirror those existing on the land.

Curtain principle

The details of trusts are kept off the register (s 27 of the LPA 1925) – beneficial interests are overreached on sale (s 2 of the LPA 1925).

Insurance principle

The accuracy of the register is guaranteed by the State, and an indemnity may be available to injured parties (see Scheds 4 and 8 to the LRA 2002).

Parts of the register

Property Register

Containing a description of the land and any benefits attached to that land; see r 5 of the LRR 2003.

- The Property Register also contains a Title Plan, which is based upon the Ordnance Survey map. The purpose of the plan is to identify the land – it rarely provides evidence of the boundaries of the estate because the register shows general boundaries only (s 60 of the LRA 2002). Application may be made by the registered proprietor to have the exact line of the boundary fixed by the Registrar (see Pt 10 of the LRR 2003).

Proprietorship Register

Containing the name of the proprietor, the class of his title and any restrictions on his title: see r 8 of the LRR 2003.

Charges Register

Containing details of any changes or incumbrances on the land: see r 9 of the LRR 2003.

In addition to the above registers, the Land Registry is required to keep the following (see Pt 2 of the LRR 2003):

- an index map, which identifies and provides the title number for each plot of registered land;

- an index of proprietors' names.

Interests in registered land

Registrable interests

Obtain their own entry on the register – their own title number, etc.

Minor interests

Entered against the relevant title – anything apart from registrable interests may be minor interests.

Overriding interests

Rights which will bind a purchaser whether they are on the register or not – for a list of overriding interests see Scheds 1 and 3 to the LRA 2002.

Registrable interests

Interests which must be registered

- Transfer of a freehold estate.

- Creation of a leasehold estate with more than seven years left to run.

- Granting of a legal charge over a freehold or leasehold for more than seven years.

See ss 4 and 27 of the LRA 2002.

Interests which may be registered

- Rentcharges;

- franchises;

- profits à prendre in gross.

See s 3 of the LRA 2002.

Classes of title

Freehold title

- Absolute title: no apparent restrictions upon applicant's title.
- Qualified title: title established for a limited period or subject to reservations.
- Possessory title: applicant in actual possession of the land.
- See s 9 of the LRA 2002.

Leasehold title

- Absolute title: no apparent restrictions upon applicant's title, or the title of the lessor.
- Good leasehold title: no apparent restrictions on the applicant's title.
- Qualified title: title established for a limited period or subject to reservations.
- Possessory title: applicant in actual possession of the land.
- See s 10 of the LRA 2002.

Minor interests: methods of protection

Notices

Agreed notices: entered with the consent of the registered proprietor:

- The entry of a notice does not mean that the interest is valid.
- May not be entered in respect of a trust of land, a leasehold estate of less than three years, or a leasehold covenant.

See ss 32–34 of the LRA 2002.

Unilateral notices: entered without the consent of the registered proprietor:

● Proprietor may apply for cancellation of the notice.

See ss 35–36 of the LRA 2002 and pt 7 of the LRA 2003.

Restrictions

● Dealings with the land must be made in accordance with any restrictions.

● A restriction may be entered, for example, when there are two registered proprietors in order to ensure that the overreaching provisions are complied with.

● See ss 40–47 of the LRA 2002.

Overriding interests

Schedule 1 to the LRA 2002 (*Rights which override first registration*)	Schedule 3 to the LRA 2002 (*Rights which override registered dispositions*)
1 Leases not exceeding seven years	1 Leases not exceeding seven years
2 An interest belonging to a person in actual occupation of the land	2 An interest belonging to a person in actual occupation of the land (see below)
3 Legal easements and profits *à prendre*	3 Legal easements and profits *à prendre* (only if the right has been used within one year of the transfer, or it is within the actual knowledge of the transferee, or it would have been discoverable on a reasonably careful inspection of the land)

4	Customary rights	4	Customary rights
5	Public rights	5	Public rights
6	Local land charges	6	Local land charges
7	Rights to coal	7	Rights to coal
8	Rights to mines and minerals created before 1898	8	Rights to mines and minerals created before 1898
9	Rights to mines and minerals created 1898–1925	9	Rights to mines and minerals created 1898–1925
10	Franchises*	10	Franchises*
11	Manorial rights*	11	Manorial rights*
12	Rights to Crown rents*	12	Rights to Crown rents*
13	Rights in respect of embankments or sea walls*	13	Rights in respect of embankments or sea walls*
14	Rights to payments in lieu of tithes*	14	Rights to payments in lieu of tithes*
15	Rights acquired by adverse possessions before 13/10/03	15	Rights acquired by adverse possessions before 13/10/03
16	Liability to repair the chancel of a church	16	Liability to repair the chancel of a church

*s 117 of the LRA 2002 provides that these rights will cease to have overriding status in 2013

Section 71(a) provides that anybody applying to register land must inform the registrar about any overriding interests of which he has knowledge. The effect of such disclosure will be that many overriding interests will be entered on the register, thereby losing their overriding status.

Paragraph 2 of Sched 3 (*the rights of persons in actual occupation*)

Does the person claiming the overriding interest have an interest in the land?

The right claimed must be an interest in the land (ie, not a licence). There can be no overriding interest if there is no interest in the first place! See *Lloyds Bank plc v Rosset* (1991). Typical interests claimed by a person in actual occupation include: beneficial interests which have been acquired informally by way of resulting or constructive trust; options to purchase the land of which he is in actual occupation; and rights to renew a lease of the land of which he is in actual occupation

---

Is the person claiming the overriding interest in actual occupation of the land at the time of the disposition?

'Actual' and 'occupation' are 'ordinary words of plain English and . . . should be interpreted as such' (Lord Wilberforce in *Williams & Glyn's Bank v Boland* (1981)).

The person claiming the interest must be in occupation of all of the land over which he claims an overriding interest because para 2 applies only 'so far as relating to land of which he is in occupation'

Did the purchaser have knowledge of that actual occupation or would it have been obvious on a reasonably careful inspection of the land?

This requirement has been added by the LRA 2002. It was not present under s 70(1)(g) of the LRA 1925 when the approach was 'if there is actual occupation and the occupier has rights, the purchaser takes subject to them. If not, he does not. No further element is material' (Lord Wilberforce in *Williams & Glyn's Bank v Boland* (1981))

↓

> **Did the purchaser make inquiries of the person in actual occupation?**
> If the purchaser made inquiries of the person in actual occupation and the person in occupation failed to declare the fact that he has an interest in the land when he could reasonably have been expected to do so, the interest of the person in actual occupation will not bind the purchaser. For this reason, mortgagees make inquiries of, and often obtain waivers from, all people in occupation of the land to be mortgaged

Many of the problems concerning people in actual occupation of land have occurred when persons in occupation have non-overreachable (one trustee) interests under resulting or constructive trusts and those interests have been held to bind a mortgagee, which has made no inquiry of the person in actual occupation. The interest in the land must have been acquired before the mortgage is granted to bind the mortgagee (*Williams & Glyn's Bank v Boland* (1981)).

If a mortgage is obtained in order to acquire the property and the beneficial interest is also created on acquisition, the person in actual occupation will usually be deemed to have given implied consent to the mortgage (*Bristol & West Building Society v Henning* (1985); *Paddington Building Society v Mendelsohn* (1985); *Abbey National Building Society v Cann* (1991)).

If an enforceable charge is redeemed using the proceeds from an unenforceable second charge, the second charge may be enforceable to the value of the first charge (*Equity & Law Home Loans Ltd v Prestidge* (1992); *Le Foe v Le Foe* (2001)).

If there are two or more trustees, the beneficial interests will be overreached on sale or mortgage (see *City of London Building Society v Flegg* (1988)).

The insurance principle – alteration of the register and indemnity

Alteration/rectification of the register

Schedule 4 to the LRA 2002

The Registrar may alter, or the court may order alteration:

- to correct a mistake;
- to bring the register up to date;
- to give effect to a right excepted from first registration.

The Registrar also has power to alter the register:

- To remove a superfluous entry.

Alteration will not be made against a proprietor in possession unless:

- the proprietor has contributed to the mistake by his fraud or lack of care; or
- it would be unjust for the alteration not to be made.

Payment of indemnity

Schedule 8 to the LRA 2002

A person may be indemnified if he has suffered loss because:

- the register has been rectified;
- there is a mistake in an official search or an official copy;
- a document kept at the Land Registry has been lost or destroyed.

No indemnity will be payable if:

- The claimant's loss results wholly from his own lack of care or wholly or partly as a result of the claimant's fraud.

A reduced indemnity may be payable:

- If the claimant's loss results partly from his own lack of care.

4 Adverse possession and boundaries

Adverse possession of land with unregistered title

A landowner can usually take action to evict a trespasser or squatter from his land. However, if he delays taking action for 12 years (unregistered land) or 10 years (registered land) he may lose the right to sue because his action will be time barred. This will effectively leave the squatter with superior title to the land.

There are two requirements that the squatter must satisfy (*Powell v McFarlane* (1977)) (refer to table oppposite):

- factual possession of the land for the limitation period; and

- *animus possidendi* (the intention to possess).

Although the squatter must not acknowledge the title of the paper owner, he may acquire title to the land by adverse possession in the following circumstances:

- When he has been in possession of the property for over 12 years but would have been willing to pay rent to the paper owner, if asked (*Lambeth LBC v Blackburn* (2001)).

- When he entered the land as a licensee and remained in possession for over 12 years after the expiration of the licence – even though he requested a renewal of the licence (*JA Pye Ltd v Graham* (2001)).

- When a tenant remained in possession for over 12 years after the expiry of the lease (*Williams v Jones* (2002)).

Factual possession	Animus possidendi
'A sufficient degree of exclusive physical control' (*Slade J in Powell v McFarlane* (1977))	'. . . the intention . . . to exclude the world at large, *including the owner with the* paper title . . . so far as is practicable and so far as the process of law will allow' (*Slade J in Powell v McFarlane* (1977))
For a period of 12 years (s 15(1) of the LA 1980)	
The type of conduct that will indicate factual possession will depend on the facts of the case and the type of land involved (*Red House Farm v Catchpole* (1977))	The squatter only has to intend to 'possess' the land; he does not have to intend to 'own' it (*Buckingham CC v Moran* (1990))
The rights of successive s quatters are cumulative (*Mount Carmel Investments Ltd v Peter Thurlow Ltd* (1988))	The squatter may claim adverse possession even though his use of the land is not inconsistent with that of the paper owner (Sched 1 to the LA 1980 and *Moran* (1990))
	The squatter should not acknowledge the paper owner's title: by offering to purchase the land (*Edginton v Clark* (1964)); or by accepting a lease of the land (*Colchester BC v Smith* (1992))
	The limitation period for Crown land is 30 years

Adverse possession of land with registered title before 13 October 2003

Before 13 October 2003 registered land was subject to the 12-year limitation period of the LA 1980 and the rules contained in the LRA 1925. Once the squatter could establish factual possession for a period of 12 years with the necessary *animus possidendi*, he had an overriding interest by virtue of s 70(1)(f) of the LRA 1925. The squatter was entitled to be entered as the proprietor and the paper owner held the property in trust for the squatter pending the latter's registration as the proprietor (s 75 of the LRA 1925). If the squatter is able to establish adverse possession for a period of 12 years, he will be subject to these rules.

In *Pye v UK* (2005) the European Court of Human Rights declared that deprivation of the paper owner without compensation could be justified in only the most exceptional circumstances, and the system of adverse possession of registered land which existed before the coming into force of the LRA 2002 breached the paper owner's right to his peaceful enjoyment of his possessions, as enshrined in art 1 of the First Protocol of the European Convention on Human Rights and Fundamental Freedoms. (See also *Beaulane Properties Ltd v Palmer* (2005)).

Adverse possession of land with registered title after 12 October 2003

Since 13 October 2003 the rules relating to the adverse possession of registered land are to be found in Sched 6 to the LRA 2002. Schedule 6 provides a new procedure which will make it considerably more difficult to acquire land by adverse possession. Some of the most important changes are as follows:

- No matter how long the duration of his adverse possession, the squatter will not acquire title to the land until he has registered his title.

- The squatter may apply to register his title after he has been in adverse possession for a period of 10 years (para 1).

- There is no special limitation period for Crown land, unless that land is foreshore when the limitation period is 60 years (para 13).

The new procedure is outlined below:

The squatter applies to the Land Registry to be registered as the proprietor of the land

The Registrar gives notice of the squatter's application to the registered proprietor and anybody else with an interest in the land (para 2). These people will then be given 65 business days to object to the registration of the squatter (para 3 and r 189 of the LRR 2003)

If there is an objection to the squatter's registration, the objector will have a period of two years to evict the squatter. If there is no objection, the squatter will be registered as the proprietor

Paragraph 5 provides that the registered proprietor will not be permitted to object if one of three conditions is satisfied:
- it would be unconscionable because of an equity by estoppel for the applicant to be dispossessed;
- the applicant is entitled to be registered as the proprietor for some reason other than his adverse possession;
- in the event of a boundary dispute, the applicant took possession of adjacent land in the reasonable belief that it belonged to him

If the registered proprietor has objected to the applicant's registration, but has not initiated proceedings to evict him, the applicant may make a further application after a further two years (para 6). The applicant will then be entitled to be registered as the proprietor (para 7)

33

Adverse possession

Possession of land with registered title

Adverse possession and leasehold land

- Adverse possession against a tenant does not operate against the landlord's title until the lease comes to an end.

- If title to the land is unregistered, the tenant may surrender the lease to the landlord who may then take possession proceedings against the squatter (*Fairweather v St Marylebone Property Trust Ltd* (1963)).

- If title to the land is registered, the tenant's surrender will not be effective and the landlord must wait until the term of the lease has ended before gaining possession. This applies whether the squatter has managed to register his title (*Spectrum Investment Co v Holmes* (1981)) or not (*Central London Commercial States Ltd v Kato Kagaku Co Ltd* (1998)).

The law of boundaries

In order to determine the boundary between two plots of land, regard may be had to the following:

- The Land Registry: usually the boundary shown on the register is a general boundary only (s 60 of the LRA 2002). However, it is possible to have the exact boundary recorded (see Pt 10 of the LRR 2003 for the procedure to be followed).

- The deeds: very often the parcels clause in the deeds will not be accurate. If the boundaries are clearly established in the deeds, that fact will usually be conclusive (*Woolls v Powling* (1999); *Burns v Morton* (1999)).

- An informal agreement between the parties to determine a boundary may be enforceable in spite of the fact that it does not comply with s 2 of the LP(MP)A 1989 (*Joyce v Rigolli* (2004)).

- Common law presumptions: the two most frequently encountered are the hedge and ditch presumption (that when plots of land are separated by a hedge and a ditch the presumption is that the boundary is the edge of the ditch farthest from the hedge – *Alan Wibberley Building Ltd v Insley* (1999)) and the *ad medium filum* rule (that, unless there is evidence to the contrary, when the boundary between two plots of land is a road or a river the presumption is that the boundary between the two plots of land runs down the centre of the road or river).

- Adverse possession: when one party has been in possession of the disputed land for the limitation period. If the land is registered and the claimant entered the land as a result of a reasonable mistake, his neighbour will have no opportunity to object to his registration as the proprietor (para 5 of Sched 6 to the LRA 2002).

- Proprietary estoppel: where the owner of disputed land permits an adjoining landowner to act to his detriment on a mistaken belief that he owns the land, the landowner may be estopped from asserting his legal rights.

- Acquiescence: a landowner should not delay in asserting his rights (*Jones v Stones* (1999)).

Party Wall etc Act 1996

- If there is no party wall between adjoining plots of land and one of the landowners wishes to construct one, he may serve notice on the adjoining landowner of his intention to build a wall (s 1). The notice period is one month. If the adjoining landowner agrees, the wall is constructed on the boundary and the expense is shared between the owners. If the adjoining owner does not consent, the wall must be built on the land of the landowner at his own expense.

- If there is already a party wall, the landowner must serve a 'party structure notice' of two months (s 3) to the adjoining landowner if he intends to strengthen, repair, underpin or demolish it. The adjoining landowner may serve a counter-notice (s 4).

- If the adjoining owner does not consent within 14 days, a dispute is deemed to have arisen (s 5).

- If any works are undertaken, the landowner must safeguard the adjoining land and, where necessary, pay compensation to the adjoining landowner (s 7).

5 Trusts of land

When trusts arise

Express trusts

- Expressly created by a settlor, who will appoint trustees, identify the beneficiaries and declare the terms of the trust.

- A declaration of trust of land must be evidenced in writing (s 53(1)(b) of the LPA 1925).

- If title to the land is registered, a restriction may be placed on the register in order to show that a trust exists.

Statutory trusts

- Whenever land is conveyed to two or more persons (ss 34–36 of the LPA 1925); when there is an intestacy (s 33 of the AEA 1925); whenever land is conveyed to a minor (s 1(6) of the LPA 1925 and s 1 of TOLATA 1996).

- If title to the land is registered, the registrar is obliged to enter a restriction on the register if he registers two or more persons as the proprietors of a registered estate (s 44 of the LRA 2002).

Implied trusts

- Trusts which are implied in certain circumstances (see resulting and constructive trusts in Chapter 6).

- Resulting and constructive trusts of land do not have to be evidenced in writing (s 53(2) of the LPA 1925).

The nature of the trust

$$S \longrightarrow \frac{\quad T1 \quad T2 \quad}{B1 \quad B2 \quad B3 \quad B4}$$

In the example above, S (the settlor) has transferred land to two trustees (T1 and T2) to hold for the benefit of four beneficiaries (B1, B2, B3 and B4).

- The settlor declares the trust and transfers the property to the trustees. Once he has constituted the trust, by transferring the property, he has no further role to play unless he is also a trustee and/or a beneficiary. A statutory trust will arise automatically if the land is conveyed to two or more people. For example, if land is conveyed to A and B, A and B will hold the land in trust for each other.

- The trustees hold the legal estate; they are the legal owners. The names of the trustees will be on the conveyance and, if title to the land is registered, the trustees will be registered at the Land Registry as the proprietors. The trustees do not own the land absolutely: they have a duty to administer the trust for the beneficiaries.

- The beneficiaries are the beneficial (or equitable) owners. They are usually entitled to occupy the property and to benefit from any rents and profits arising from the land. They will be entitled to the proceeds if the land is sold. Their interests may be concurrent or successive.

- Concurrent interests occur when all of the beneficiaries are entitled to benefit at the same time. For example, if S has transferred land to his trustees to hold for the benefit of his four nephews, this creates concurrent interests, or co-ownership. The beneficiaries are all entitled to benefit from the trust immediately.

- If we imagine that B1 is S's wife and B2, B3 and B4 are the children from a previous marriage, S may wish to declare a trust in his will by which he leaves the land to B1 for life with remainder, after B1's death, to B2, B3 and B4. If he does so he creates successive interests. B1 (known as the life tenant) will be entitled to enjoy the property for as long as she lives, and then the other beneficiaries (beneficiaries in remainder) will become entitled to benefit from the land when she dies.

Trusts of land

39

The nature of the trust

Trusts of land before 1997

There were two types of trusts:

- Strict settlements under the SLA 1925 dealt only with successive interests. The legal estate was held by the tenant for life, who held the land for the beneficiaries in remainder. It has not been possible to create any new strict settlements (s 2 of TOLATA 1996) or entailed interests (Sched 1) since the beginning of 1997. Settlements created before 1997 continue to exist, however.

- Trusts for sale under the LPA 1925 dealt with both successive and concurrent interests. The legal estate was held by the trustees, who held the land for the benefit of the beneficiaries. Sections 4 and 5 of TOLATA 1996 effectively turn all trusts for sale into trusts of land after 1996.

Trusts of land after 1996

- Since 1 January 1997, it has been possible to create only one type of trust of land. Section 1 of TOLATA 1996 provides that '"trust of land" means . . . any trust which consists of or includes land . . .'.

The legal estate

- The legal estate is held by the trustees.

- There must not be more than four trustees (s 34(2) of the LPA 1925 and s 34(2) of the TA 1925).

- If land is conveyed to more than four people and the trustees have not been nominated, the first four named will be the trustees.

- The legal estate is always held as a joint tenancy, with a right of survivorship (*jus accrescendi*).

- The legal joint tenancy can never be severed to form a tenancy in common (s 1(6) and s 36(2) of the LPA 1925).

For example, A, B, C and D hold the legal estate of a plot of land:

A	B	C	D

If C dies, A, B and D continue to hold the legal estate:

A	B	D

The powers of the trustees

- The trustees have all the powers of an absolute owner (s 6(1) of TOLATA 1996).
- The trustees may partition the land (s 7 of TOLATA 1996).
- The trustees may delegate any of their functions by power of attorney to any beneficiary of full age who has an interest in possession in the land (s 8 of TOLATA 1996).
- The trustees may be required by the trust instrument to obtain consent before exercising any of their powers (s 10 of TOLATA 1996).
- In exercising their functions, trustees must, so far as practicable, consult all of the beneficiaries who are of full age and beneficially entitled to an interest in possession of the land. They should, so far as consistent with the general interest of the trust, give effect to the wishes of the majority (according to the value of their combined interests (s 11 of TOLATA 1996)).

The beneficial interests

Beneficial interests may be held either jointly or in common. Unless there is evidence to the contrary, the presumption will be that 'equity follows the law' and that the beneficial interests are held as a joint tenancy (see *Supperstone v Hurst* (2005)). For example, if land is conveyed to A, B, C, D, E and F, the legal estate will be held by the first four named (s 34(2) of the LPA 1925), but they all have a beneficial interest.

If C dies:

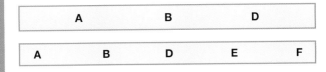

The beneficial tenancy in common

Unlike the legal estate, which must be held as a joint tenancy (s 1(6) of the LPA 1925), a beneficial interest may be held in common (otherwise known as an undivided share). Each beneficial tenant in common has his own share of the property and the right of survivorship will not apply. For example:

If C dies, his share will not be taken by the other tenants in common. C may leave his share to somebody by will or it will devolve according to the rules of intestacy if he does not make a will. In this case, he has left it to X:

As a tenant in common, C may also sell or give away his share whilst he is still alive. If he does so, he will remain a trustee until he dies or retires from office:

Creation of a tenancy in common

A joint tenancy is characterised by the four unities (*AG Securities v Vaughan* (1990)). If any of the four unities are absent, there cannot be a joint tenancy. The four unities are:

- Unity of possession – all joint tenants must be equally entitled to possession of the land.
- Unity of interest – all joint tenants must have the same interest in the land.
- Unity of time – all joint tenants must have acquired title to the land at the same time.
- Unity of title – each co-owner must claim title under the same document.

A tenancy in common may be created expressly by using 'words of severance' in the conveyance. Examples of words of severance include: 'equally'; 'in equal shares'; 'to be divided between'; 'between'; 'amongst'; 'in equal moieties'. In the example above, the words 'to A, B, C, D, E and F in equal shares' would create a tenancy in common.

Words of severance are unlikely to be conclusive in registered land because the form of transfer (Form TR1) requires transferees to state whether they are to hold the land as joint tenants or as tenants in common.

A tenancy in common will also be presumed in the following circumstances:

- Commercial partners who acquire property together (*Lake v Craddock* (1955)).

- Purchasers who contribute in unequal shares (*Bull v Bull* (1955)).

- Business tenants (*Malayan Credit Ltd v Jack Chia-MPH Ltd* (1986)).

- Mortgagees between themselves (*Petty v Styward* (1631)).

Severance

A joint tenant may turn his joint tenancy into a tenancy in common by a process known as severance (s 36(2) of the LPA 1925). In the example below, C has severed his interest, thereby creating a tenancy in common of his share. The others remain as joint tenants:

Because of the effect of severance, it is not possible to sever a joint tenancy by will – it must take effect *inter vivos*. If it was possible to sever by will, it would be possible for C to defraud his co-owners by agreeing with them to hold the property as a joint tenancy. C could then execute a will which severed the joint tenancy posthumously, thereby defrauding the other co-owners. In such a situation C could not lose: if his co-owners died first, C would obtain their shares by survivorship; but if C died first, the co-owners would find out after his death that they were not to benefit from C's death. The rule against severance by will can have serious implications for solicitors when drafting wills (*Carr-Glynn v Frearsons* (1998)).

Methods of severance

- By written notice (s 36(2) and s 196 of the LPA 1925). The notice must be 'left at' the last known place of abode or business of the other joint tenants (s 196(3)) or may be sent by recorded or special delivery (s 196(4)). A notice sent by ordinary first class post will be sufficient, provided that it is delivered – it has therefore been 'left at' the address, and it does not matter whether the intended recipient actually sees the notice (*Kinch v Bullard* (1999)). A notice sent by recorded delivery will be 'deemed to be made at the time at which the registered letter would in the ordinary course be delivered' (s 196(4) and *WX Investments v Begg* (2002)), and it does not matter whether or not the intended recipient actually receives it (*Re 88 Berkeley Road, London NW9* (1983)).

- By a joint tenant acting upon his own share (selling or mortgaging it – see *First National Securities Ltd v Hegerty* (1985)).

- By mutual agreement (*Burgess v Rawnsley* (1975)).

- By mutual conduct (*Williams v Hensman* (1975)).

- By the bankruptcy of a joint tenant (*Re Dennis* (1995)).

- By merger of interest (one joint tenant acquires the interest of another).

- By forfeiture – when one joint tenant kills another, he may be prohibited from benefiting from his unlawful conduct (*In the Estate of Crippen* (1911)). The forfeiture rule may, in certain circumstances, be modified by the court if the offender is guilty of manslaughter, but not if he is guilty of murder (s 2 of the Forfeiture Act 1982 and *Re K* (1986)).

- By operation of law (for example, the Inheritance (Provision for Family and Dependants) Act 1975).

When a joint tenancy is severed it always severs in equal shares (*Nielson-Jones v Fedden* (1975)). However, if there has been an express declaration regarding shares, the declaration will usually be conclusive (*Goodman v Gallant* (1986)). If there is no express declaration, the court may take all of the circumstances of the case into consideration when apportioning shares (*Bernard v Josephs* (1982)).

Section 24 of the Matrimonial Causes Act 1973 gives the court discretion to vary property rights on divorce.

Rights of the beneficiaries

Section 12(1) of TOLATA 1996 gives the beneficiaries a right to occupy the land provided that:

- his occupation is within the purposes of the trust; and
- the land is held by the trustees so as to be available.

Section 13 provides that where there are two or more beneficiaries who are entitled to occupy the land, the trustees may allow one or more of them to occupy the land, or part of it, and to restrict the rights of the other beneficiaries (see *Rodway v Landy* (2001)). The trustees must not unreasonably restrict a beneficiary's right of occupation (s 13(2)). A beneficiary in occupation may be required to pay compensation to an excluded beneficiary (s 13(6)). When deciding whether to exercise their powers of exclusion or restriction the trustees are directed to have regard to (s 13(4)):

- the intention of the person (if any) who created the trust;
- the purposes for which the property is held;

- the circumstances and wishes of each of the beneficiaries who is entitled to occupy the land.

Sale of the trust land

The interests of the beneficiaries are overreached on sale provided that the capital money is paid to, and a receipt obtained from, the trustees, being at least two in number or a trust corporation (ss 2 and 27 of the LPA 1925).

Section 14 of TOLATA 1996 provides that any person interested (trustee, beneficiary, mortgagee, etc) may apply to the court for an order:

- relating to the exercise by trustees of any of their functions (including the exercise of their power of sale); or

- declaring the nature or extent of a person's interest under the trust.

Very often the dispute will arise when one or more of the persons interested wants to sell the land but others do not.

Under s 14, the court may make 'such order as the court thinks fit'.

When determining an application for an order under s 14, the matters to which the court is to have regard include those listed in s 15:

- the intentions of the person or persons who created the trust (s 15(1)(a));

- the purposes for which the property is held (s 15(1)(b));

- the welfare of any minor who occupies or might reasonably be expected to occupy the property as his home (s 15(1)(c));

- the interests of any secured creditor of any beneficiary (s 15(1)(d));

- the circumstances and wishes of any beneficiaries of full age and entitled to an interest in possession or, in the case of dispute, to the majority (according to their combined interests) (s 15(3)).

Before 1997 (when applications were brought under s 30 of the LPA 1925), there was presumption in favour of sale but the courts would not order sale when there was a collateral purpose (*Re Buchanan-Wollaston's Conveyance* (1939); *Abbey National plc v Moss* (1994)) until that purpose had ended (*Jones v Challenger* (1961)). Since TOLATA came into force, there has been no presumption in favour of sale, and the old cases, though often useful, 'should be treated with caution' (*Mortgage Corp Ltd v Shaire* (2001)).

Section 15 does not apply in insolvency, which is governed by s 335A of the Insolvency Act 1986. After one year of the bankrupt's estate vesting in the trustee in bankruptcy, the court is directed to assume that the interests of the bankrupt's creditors outweigh all other considerations, unless the circumstances of the case are exceptional. For an example of a case involving exceptional circumstances, see *Re Holliday* (1981).

Termination of a trust of land

This occurs:

- when the land is sold;
- when one beneficiary acquires the entire beneficial interest. This may occur by survivorship or by one beneficiary purchasing the shares of the other beneficiaries;
- by partition of the land. Each beneficiary will receive his own deeds (unregistered land) or registered title (registered land).

6 Resulting trusts, constructive trusts, proprietary estoppel and licences

A declaration of trust of land should be evidenced in writing (s 53(1)(b) of the LPA 1925). However, it is possible to acquire an interest in land without any formalities by way of resulting or constructive trusts (s 53(2)) or by way of proprietary estoppel.

Resulting trusts

- A resulting trust of land arises by way of presumption. The presumption is raised by contributions towards the purchase price of the land. Contributions made by way of mortgage loan may give rise to the presumption, but, since *Curley v Parkes* (2004) it appears that mortgage repayments which are made after acquisition may give rise to a constructive, rather than a resulting, trust.

- A right-to-buy discount may count as a contribution (*Springette v Defoe* (1992)).

- The presumption may be rebutted if the contributions were intended to be a gift or a loan.

- The presumption of advancement (that contributions from husband to wife or from father to child are presumed to be gifts) may also apply. However, the current status of the presumption of advancement is questionable (see *Pettitt v Pettitt* (1970)).

- A beneficiary under a resulting trust has an interest in the land in proportion to his contributions.

Constructive trusts

- Anybody claiming an interest in land by way of constructive trust must satisfy three requirements (*Lloyds Bank plc v Rosset* (1991)):

- a common intention that they were to benefit;

- detrimental reliance upon the common intention;

- unconscionability or equitable fraud on the part of the legal owner.

- A beneficiary under a constructive trust of land has an interest in the land. The court may take into account all the circumstances of a case when quantifying the extent of that interest – a 'broad brush' approach (*Drake v Whipp* (1995); *Oxley v Hiscock* (2004).

- The 'broad brush' approach to quantification has been used when the claimant appears to have acquired an interest by way of *resulting* trust (*Midland Bank v Cooke* (1995); *Le Foe v Le Foe* (2001); *Oxley v Hiscock* (2004)).

- A constructive trust of land may also arise when one party acquires land from another expressly 'subject to' a prior agreement (*Binions v Evans* (1972); *Lyus v Prowsa Developments Ltd* (1982)).

A common intention may be established or evidenced by:

- evidence of an express agreement; or

- contributions after the acquisition of the property (*Hussey v Palmer* (1972)), or perhaps even at the time of acquisition (*Oxley v Hiscock* (2004)). The contributions must be referable to the realty (*Burns v Burns* (1984)), but contributions by themselves are not sufficient – they must evidence a common intention (*Thomas v Fuller-Brown* (1988));

- 'regular substantial mortgage repayments' (Lord Diplock in *Gissing v Gissing* (1971); *Curley v Parkes* (2004); or

- an 'express promise' by the legal owner – *Eves v Eves* (1975) (assurance by a man that house would be in joint names if his partner was 21); *Grant v Edwards* (1986) (excuse made by man that the woman's name had to be kept off the title deeds to prevent her husband obtaining an interest in the property on divorce); *Hammond v Mitchell* (1991) ('when we are married the house will be half yours anyway').

Purchase of land subject to resulting or constructive trusts

- A purchaser of the legal estate will take the land free from interests under a trust provided that he obtains a receipt from the trustees, being at least two in number or a trust corporation (ss 2 and 27 of the LPA 1925; *City of London Building Society v Flegg* (1988)).

- If the land is unregistered, a non-overreachable interest will bind a purchaser if he has notice, actual or constructive, of that interest (*Kingsnorth Finance Co Ltd v Tizard* (1986)).

- If title to the land is registered, a non-overreachable interest will bind a purchaser if the owner of the interest is in actual occupation of the land and the circumstances satisfy the requirements of para 2 of Sched 3 (or Sched 1 if the land is subject to first registration) to the LRA 2002.

Proprietary estoppel

The modern definition of proprietary estoppel was given by Lord Oliver in *Taylor's Fashions Ltd v Liverpool Victoria Trustees Co Ltd* (1982). An equity by estoppel will arise when it would be 'unconscionable for a party to be permitted to deny that which, knowingly or unknowingly, he has allowed another to assume to his detriment'. The test is therefore one of unconscionability which will arise when the following factors are present:

- promise, assurance, representation or acquiescence on the part of the legal owner;

- detriment;

- reliance.

The elements of reliance and detriment are often intertwined and the court is to 'look at the matter in the round' (*Gillett v Holt* (2000)). The remedy awarded to a successful claimant will be 'the minimum equity to do justice' (*Baker v Baker* (1993)): it may amount to a freehold estate in the land (*Pascoe v Turner* (1979)); a right to occupy a property for life (*Greasley v Cooke* (1980)); a right of access (*Crabb v Arun DC* (1976)); or a right of way (*ER Ives v High* (1967)).

Section 116 of the LRA 2002 confirms that, in relation to registered land, an equity by estoppel is capable of binding successors in title. The claimant may therefore enter his interest as a notice at the Land Registry or, if in actual occupation, claim an overriding interest. The status of the right in unregistered land depends upon the doctrine of notice (*ER Ives v High* (1967)).

The rights compared

Resulting trust	Constructive trust	Proprietary estoppel
Requires: Presumption raised by a contribution made at the time of acquisition The presumption may be rebutted if the contribution was a gift or a loan	*Requires*: Common intention Reliance Detriment Unconscionability	*Requires*: Assurance, representation or acquiescence Reliance Detriment Unconscionability
Remedy: An interest in proportion to the contribution	*Remedy*: The 'broad bush' approach	*Remedy*: The minimum equity to do justice

Since *Oxley v Hiscock* (2004) it appears that the courts will look for evidence of a common intention in order to find a constructive trust, even if the evidence of the constructive trust is to be found in contributions made at the time of acquisition. The resulting trust will therefore only be relevant if it is not possible to infer a common intention from such contributions (see *Curley v Parkes* (2004)).

There are obvious similarities between constructive trusts and proprietary estoppel and it has long since been recognised that in some circumstances an interest could arise by either method (see *Grant v Edwards* (1986)). More controversially, in *Oxley v Hiscock* (2004), Chadwick LJ considered that in cohabitation cases there is little, if any, difference in outcome between constructive trusts and proprietary estoppel.

Licences

A licence is merely a permission to do something on the land or to occupy it. It is not an interest in the land, even if it involves occupation of land for many years.

Licences may be divided into four categories:

Bare licence

A bare licence is a mere permission to do something on land which, without permission, would be a trespass. A typical example occurs when a landowner permits a child to retrieve a lost ball from his garden.

A bare licence may be revoked at will.

Licence coupled with an interest

Typically, the interest will be a contractual right or a profit *à prendre*. For example, if a landowner makes a contract with somebody to cut and take away timber from his land (*James*

Jones Ltd v Earl of Tankerville (1909)), or grants him a profit of estovers (right to take wood), he must be impliedly granting him a licence to enter his land in order to exercise the benefit of the contract or profit.

In this case, the licence will usually be irrevocable throughout the period of the grant or contractual term.

Contractual licence

A contractual licence is simply a licence which has been granted by valid contract. Termination of the licence is only possible within the terms of the contract. If there is no express provision in the contract, reasonable notice must be given to terminate the licence (*Winter Garden Theatre Ltd v Millennium Productions Ltd* (1948)).

A contractual licence generally does not bind third parties (*King v David Allen Ltd* (1916), but see also *Errington v Errington and Woods* (1952)).

A contractual licence is not an interest in the land and cannot be an overriding interest (*Ashburn Anstalt v Arnold* (1989)).

Estoppel licence

An estoppel licence is a licence which has been acquired by proprietary estoppel (see above for proprietary estoppel)

Constructive trusts

7 Leases

A lease is also known as a term of years, a demise or a tenancy. Whatever term is used, it is the second legal estate in land (s 1(1) of the LPA 1925).

The concept of the lease

Section 205(1)(xxvii) of the LPA 1925 defines a lease. It is an estate in the land for a fixed maximum term, which may be of any duration from one week (or even less) to 3,000 years (or even more). Typically, a long lease will be granted by a landlord (lessor) to a tenant (lessee) who will pay a lump sum (or premium) and a small amount of periodic rent (eg, it may be as little as a peppercorn annually). Short leases may not involve the payment of a premium, but will usually involve the payment of rent periodically.

Terminology

Term	Example
Leases: in this example, A, the freeholder, has granted a lease for 999 years to B. B and his successors will go into possession of the land for 999 years, after which time the lease will determine (terminate). After 999 years, A's successor will be able to recover possession. The landlord is said to hold the reversion because the property will revert back to him when the lease ends.	**A** Landlord (freehold estate) ↓ (999 years) **B** Tenant (leasehold estate)

Subleases: in this example, A has granted a lease for a term of 999 years to B, who sublets the property to C for 99 years, who sublets to D for 9 years. A sublease may be of any period provided that it is shorter than the superior lease by at least one day. A is the landlord of the head lease (the superior lease) and D is the tenant under the final sublease. B is the tenant under the 999-year lease and the landlord of the 99-year lease. Similarly, C is the tenant under the 99-year lease and the landlord of the 9-year lease.	**A** The lessor or landlord ↓ (999 years) **B** A's tenant – also C's landlord ↓ (99 years) **C** B's tenant – also D's landlord ↓ (9 years) **D** The sublessee or subtenant
Assignments: in contrast to a sublease, an assignment occurs when the whole of an interest is transferred. In this case, A has granted a 999-year lease to B and has then assigned his reversion to Y, who is now the landlord. B has also assigned the lease to X, who is now the tenant.	**A → Y** assignment of the reversion) ↓ (999 years) **B → X** (assignment of the lease)

Types of lease

- Fixed term leases: the lease is granted for a fixed period (1,000 years, 10 years, etc). The lease will determine when the period comes to an end.

- Yearly tenancies: yearly tenancies may be created expressly or by the tenant going into possession and paying rent calculated by reference to a year. The lease continues from year to year until notice is given. Unless agreed to the contrary, the notice period is usually six months.

- Legal periodic tenancies: legal periodic tenancies may be created either expressly or by the tenant going into possession and offering rent. If no term is specified, the term will be the period by which rent is calculated – for example, rent of £1,200 per year, payable monthly, creates a yearly, rather than a monthly, tenancy. If no term is agreed but rent has been offered and accepted, the term will be one rental period. Legal periodic tenancies determine when one party serves a notice to quit. In the absence of a contrary agreement, the notice period should be one full term. Residential tenants should generally be given at least four weeks' notice (s 5 of the PEA 1977) unless they are excluded tenants under the HA 1988 and they have agreed to the contrary with the landlord. The tenant will often enjoy some form of statutory protection (see p. 62).

- Tenancies at will: tenancies at will arise when a tenant occupies land as a tenant subject to an agreement with the landlord that either party may determine the tenancy at any time. A classic example of a tenancy at will occurs when a landlord permits a tenant into occupation whilst negotiations for an agreement are proceeding (see *Javad v Aqil* (1991)). The status of a tenancy at will is uncertain: the tenant has no estate in the land and his rights are more akin to those of a licensee.

- Tenancies at sufferance: tenancies at sufferance occur when a tenant, without the landlord's consent or dissent, holds over at the end of a leasehold term. A tenant at sufferance is not a trespasser (he entered the land with permission), nor is he a tenant (his tenancy has ceased); his status is more akin to a squatter. If the landlord assents to his occupation, the tenant at sufferance will become a tenant at will.

Creation of leases and statutory formalities

Legal leases

- *Term over three years*: must be made by deed (s 52(1) of the LPA 1925).

- *Three years or less*: may be created by parol (s 54(2) of the LPA 1925).

- *Assignments of leases*: must be made by deed regardless of the term. (*Crago v Julien* (1992))

Equitable leases

Require a valid contract: s 2 of the LP(MP)A 1989 or s 40 of the LPA 1925 if created before 26 September 1989.

Such a lease is known as a lease under the rule in *Walsh v Lonsdale* (1882). It is not really a lease: it is a contract to create a lease, but equity reads the agreement as a lease because 'equity sees as done that which ought to be done' and may grant specific performance of the contract.

Tenancies by estoppel

When a landlord and tenant have purported to create a valid lease, the landlord may not deny the title of the tenant and the tenant may not deny the title of his landlord. If the landlord did not have the legal estate when he purportedly granted the lease but he subsequently acquires it, the estoppel is said to have been 'fed' and the tenant will acquire a lease as soon as the landlord acquires the estate.

Tenancies acquired by proprietary estoppel

A lease may be created without formalities when the tenant has acted to his detriment in reliance upon a promise or representation which has been made to him by the landowner (see *Yaxley v Gotts* (2000))

Protection of the lease against purchasers

Registered land

- *Legal leases over seven years and assignments with more than seven years left to run*: these are registrable estates at the Land Registry (s 4 of the LRA 2002). Before 13 October 2003, the qualifying period was 21 years.

- *Legal leases for seven years or less*: these are overriding interests (para 1 to Scheds 1 and 3 to the LRA 2002).

- *Equitable leases*: these should be entered as a notice against the lessor's title, though they may be overriding interests if the lessee remains in actual occupation (para 2 of Scheds 1 and 3 to the LRA 2002).

Unregistered land

- *Legal leases*: these are rights *in rem* which do not require protection.

- *Equitable leases*: these should be entered as estate contracts (Class C(iv) land charge) in the Land Charges Register (s 2(4) of the LCA 1972).

Statutory protection for periodic tenants

Because periodic tenants depend on renewal of their tenancies, their status is rather precarious. The landlord may evict them at common law by serving a valid notice to quit. Some tenants may be able to claim statutory protection:

- *Business tenants* may be able to claim the protection of Part II of the Landlord and Tenant Act 1954. The Act provides for limited security of tenure, and may be excluded.

- *Agricultural tenants* may be subject to the Agricultural Holdings Act 1986 or the Agricultural Tenancies Act 1995. Both Acts provide limited security of tenure.

- *Residential tenants* may be subject to one of the following:
  - The Rent Act 1977 (protected tenancies) applies to private residential tenancies created before 15 January 1989. The landlord needs adequate grounds to evict the tenant, who also has the benefit of rent control.
  - The Housing Act 1985 (secure tenancies) provides security of tenure to public sector tenants.
  - The Housing Act 1988 (assured tenancies) applies to private residential tenancies created after 14 January 1989. In its original form the 1988 Act curtailed the statutory scheme of the 1977 Act and introduced the assured shorthold tenancy, which enabled the landlord to recover possession easily and quickly. Since the Housing Act 1996, all tenancies take effect as shortholds unless the parties expressly choose to create an assured tenancy.

Essential requirements for a lease

In addition to the formality and registration requirements, a lease has certain distinguishing characteristics. These were identified by Lord Templeman in *Street v Mountford* (1985) as being 'exclusive possession for a fixed or periodic term certain in consideration of a premium or periodic payments'. In other words the three requirements are: exclusive possession; for a term certain; at a rent or premium. To deal with the requirements in reverse order:

Rent or premium

Section 205(1)(xxvii) defines a lease as taking effect 'whether or not at a rent' and it is possible to create a rent-free lease (see *Ashburn Anstalt v Arnold* (1989) and *Ingram v IRC* (1999)). However, the absence of rent usually indicates that the occupier occupies the property as a licensee rather than as a tenant.

If rent is paid, it must be a fixed sum and not a fluctuating amount (*Bostock v Bryant* (1990)).

Term certain

A lease must have a fixed maximum duration. The agreement may contain a break clause (eg, a 20-year lease with an option to determine every five years) or a provision which determines the lease upon the happening of a particular event, but the maximum duration must be known at the outset. For this reason there could not be a lease when property was let 'for the duration' of the war in *Lace v Chantler* (1944). In *Prudential Assurance Co v London Residuary Body* (1992), there was held to be no lease until Walworth Road was required for widening, but the tenant was deemed to have a yearly tenancy because rent had been offered and accepted on that basis.

Exclusive possession

The occupier must have control over the property (*National Car Parks Ltd v Trinity Development Co Ltd* (2001)) and must be able to exclude the landlord. Certain categories of people will not be tenants even if they have exclusive occupation of the property. Such categories include:

- Tenants at will

- Tenants at sufferance

- Tolerated trespassers – when a public sector landlord permits an ex-tenant to remain in occupation even though a possession order has been made against the ex-tenant, the ex-tenant remains in occupation as a tolerated trespasser (*Stirling v. Leadenhall Residential 2 Ltd* (2001); he does not become tenant even if he pays rent and it is accepted (*Newham L.B.C. v. Hawkins* (2005) unless the landlord offers a new tenancy agreement (*Swindon B.C. v. Aston* (2002)

- Service occupiers who occupy for the better performance of their duties (*Norris v Checksfield* (1991) – coach mechanic and chauffeur; *Surrey CC v Lamond* (1998) – school caretaker)

- Occupation based on acts of charity, generosity or friendship (*Facchini v Bryson* (1952); *Marcroft Wagons Ltd v Smith* (1951); *Gray v Taylor* (1998))

- Occupiers who have services provided for them (*Otter v Norman* (1989) – a continental breakfast)

- Lodgers – people with a resident landlord (*Street v Mountford* (1985); *Mortgage Corp Ltd v Ubah* (1997))

The lease/licence distinction

Because of the protection given to tenants by the RA 1977, landlords attempted to evade the RA, which applied only to tenancies, by purporting to grant licences instead of leases. Landlords sought to grant licences by denying exclusive possession to occupiers.

The distinction is less important for tenancies created since the HA 1988 because landlords are now able to recover possession at the end of the term by granting assured shorthold tenancies. Nevertheless, the cases that came before the courts on the RA 1977 have provided our modern definition of a lease:

- *Somma v Hazelhurst and Savelli* (1978): the landlord was deemed to be able to grant a licence to two occupiers simply by calling the agreement a licence. The fact that the agreement included a sham clause allowing the licensor or anybody nominated by him to share with the couple was deemed to be irrelevant.

- *Street v Mountford* (1985): the House of Lords overruled *Somma*. Lord Templeman stated that if a landlord grants exclusive possession, for a term certain, at a rent or premium, he has created a lease, notwithstanding the fact that the agreement is termed a licence. The court should 'be astute to frustrate sham devices and artificial transactions whose only object is to disguise the grant of a tenancy and to evade the Rent Acts' (see also *Aslan v Murphy* (1990) – the landlord kept a key and denied possession to the tenant between the hours of 10.30 and 12 noon each day).

- When there is more than one occupant, the issue is one of fact, depending upon the nature of the accommodation and the relationship between the occupiers (*Stribling v Wickham* (1989)). As a rough rule of thumb, if the occupiers are jointly liable for the whole of the rent a joint tenancy (lease) exists; if the occupants are liable only for their 'share' of the rent they are probably licensees (*Mikeover v Brady* (1989)). The House of Lords decided in *AG Securities v Vaughan* (1992) that, in order for a joint tenancy to exist, the four unities must be present: unity of possession, interest, time and title. In *Vaughan*, Lord Oliver found that none of the unities was present and that 'each person is individually liable for his own rent, which may differ in practice from the amounts paid by all or one of the others . . .'.

- In *Antoniades v Villiers* (1992), the House of Lords decided that two occupants of a bed-sitting room were tenants despite the fact that they were, in theory, each liable for their own rent. As Lord Oliver explained, the presumption as to rent 'rest[s] upon the assumption that the licences are not sham documents, which is the very question in issue'.

- One successful method used by landlords to avoid the Rent Acts is letting only to a company. Company lets are subject to Pt II of the LTA 1954, rather than the RA 1977 (*Hilton v Plustitle* (1988); *Eaton Square Properties Ltd v O'Higgins* (2000)).

Social housing

There have been a number of decisions in recent years concerning tenancies or licences of social housing. They include:

- *Family Housing Association v Jones* (1990): provision of temporary accommodation at less than market rent created a tenancy.

- *Westminster CC v Clarke* (1992): the House of Lords held that an occupant of a bedsit in a hostel for single homeless men, who could be moved to another room without notice, was a licensee.

- *Gray v Taylor* (1998): an occupant of almshouses who paid towards her upkeep was held to be a licensee.

- *Bruton v London and Quadrant Housing Trust* (1999): the House of Lords held that an occupant of temporary housing for the homeless was a tenant for the purposes of s 11 of the LTA 1985 in spite of the fact that the 'landlord' was only a licensee. If the grantor did not have a legal estate in the land, how is it possible for him to grant a lease to the grantee (*nemo dat quod non habet*)? Lord Hoffmann decided that the occupant was a tenant because he had exclusive possession for a term at a rent, but that his lease would not bind third parties. The decision appears to create a new type of interest – a non-proprietary lease. As Martin Dixon has observed ([2000] CLJ 28) 'Lord Hoffmann's explanation of why the contractual arrangement between Bruton and the trust can be regarded as a lease, even though the trust has no estate in the land, is actually an explanation of why it is a contractual licence'.

- *Uratemp Ventures Ltd v Collins* (2001): the House of Lords held that an occupant of a room in a hotel was capable of being a tenant of a 'separate dwelling' for the purposes of the HA 1988.

Leasehold covenants

Leasehold covenants are promises contained in leases by which one party undertakes to do something or not do something. Some covenants are implied; others may be express:

- *The tenant's implied obligations*: keeping property in 'a tenant-like manner' (*Marden v Heyes Ltd* (1972)); to allow the landlord to enter and inspect the property (*Mint v Good*

(1951)); to pay rent, rates and taxes (*United Scientific Holdings v Burnley BC* (1977)).

- *The landlord's implied obligations*: to permit the tenant 'quiet enjoyment' of the premises – not to harass or interfere with the tenant's enjoyment (*McCall v Abelesz* (1976)); not to derogate from grant (*Stewart v Scottish Widows & Life Assurance plc* (2005); to ensure that dwelling houses are reasonably fit for human habitation (s 8 of the LTA 1985); to keep in repair the structure of a dwelling house let for a term of less than seven years (s 1 of the LTA 1985).

- *Express covenants*: there are many different types of covenant – two of the most common being the tenant covenanting not to assign or sublet the lease, or the landlord covenanting to repair the property.

Enforcing covenants in leases created before 1 January 1996

- The original landlord and tenant would be in privity of contract and could therefore sue each other on the contract.

- The original tenant may be liable throughout the original term of the lease, even after he has assigned the lease (*City of London Corp v Fell* (1993)). The original tenant may be able to recover from the defaulting tenant under the rule in *Moule v Garrett* (1872), or from the person to whom he directly assigned the lease under s 77 of the LPA 1925.

- The original landlord may also be liable throughout the term of the lease, even after assignment of the reversion (*Stuart v Joy* (1904)).

- Assignees will also generally be liable if they are in privity of estate (*Spencer's Case* (1583)) and the covenant 'touches and concerns the land' (*P & A Swift v Combines English Stores Group* (1989)).

● The LPA 1925 provides that the benefit (s 141) and burden (s 142) of the landlord's covenants will pass with the reversion.

● The burden of negative covenants may be enforced under the rule in *Tulk v Moxhay* (1848).

Enforcing covenants in leases created after 31 December 1995

● The LT(C)A 1995 applies to all landlord and tenant covenants (s 2(1)).

● The benefit and burden of all covenants, legal and equitable, will pass on assignment of the land (s 3), unless the covenants are expressed to be personal (s 3(6)).

● The benefit of a landlord's right of re-entry will also pass (s 4).

● A tenant is released from the burden and ceases to be entitled to the benefit of his covenants when he assigns the lease (s 5).

● The tenant may be required to guarantee performance of the covenants by his assignee (s 16). This is known as an authorised guarantee agreement (AGA).

● A landlord (s 6) or former landlord (s 7) may apply to be released from the benefit and burden of his covenants if he assigns the reversion. Any objection to release must be reasonable (s 8).

Landlord's remedies for breach of covenant

● *Action for arrears of rent:* there is a six-year limitation period (s 19 of the LA 1980).

● Damages.

- *Injunction and specific performance*: specific performance will only be granted if it would not be oppressive to the tenant and the rules of equity have been satisfied (*Co-operative Insurance Society Ltd v Argyll Stores Ltd* (1998)). Specific performance of a repairing covenant will only be available in exceptional circumstances (*Rainbow Estates Ltd v Tokenhold* (1999)).

- *Distress (or distraint)*: distress occurs when a landlord enters the demised premises and seizes the tenant's goods in satisfaction of rent arrears. A landlord should take great care before exercising this ancient remedy which, though draconian, does not infringe the European Convention on Human Rights (*Fuller v Happy Shopper Markets Ltd* (2001)).

- *Forfeiture*: if the lease contains a right of re-entry, the landlord may be able to resort to the remedy of forfeiture if the tenant breaches his covenants. The landlord may forfeit the lease either by peaceable re-entry or by bringing possession proceedings, although only the latter method is possible for residential property (s 2 of PEA 1977). If the breach of covenant is for non-payment of rent, the landlord must comply with the procedure outlined in the Common Law Procedure Act 1852. In all other circumstances he must comply with s 146 of the LPA 1925. The court has discretion to grant relief to the tenant even after the landlord has succeeded in re-entering the premises (*Billson v Residential Apartments Ltd* (1992)).

Tenant's remedies for breach of covenant

- *Damages*: the tenant is entitled to be placed in the position he would have been in had there been no breach (*Calabar Properties Ltd v Stitcher* (1984)).

- *Injunction and specific performance*: specific performance of a landlord's covenant to repair is generally available to the tenant (s 17 of the LTA 1985 and *Jeune v Queens Cross Properties* (1974)).

- *Retention of rent to pay for repairs (equitable set-off)*: if the landlord takes action against the tenant for non-payment of rent and the landlord has breached his covenants to repair, the tenant may be entitled to set off the value of the repairs against his rent arrears (*Eller v Grovecrest Investments Ltd* (1995)).

Methods of terminating leases

Effluxion of time

The period of the lease comes to an end. The tenant may have statutory protection, however.

Forfeiture

See above.

Notice to quit

A valid notice may be served by one of a number of joint tenants (*Hammersmith & Fulham LBC v Monk* (1992) and *Notting Hill Housing Trust v Brackley* (2001)). Notices used to have to be correct in every detail in order to be effective but, since *Mannai Investment Co v Eagle Star Life Assurance Co Ltd* (1997), minor discrepancies may be disregarded if a reasonable recipient would have realised the intended effect of the notice. The decision in *Mannai* appears to have caused a great deal of uncertainty (see Diamond and Sandham (2004) *Conv* 361).

Surrender

The tenant surrenders his lease to the landlord who accepts the surrender.

Merger

The tenant acquires the landlord's reversion, thereby merging it with the lease.

Disclaimer

The tenant denies his landlord's title.

Enlargement

When a tenant holds a lease which was originally granted for 300 years or more and there are still 200 years or more left to run, he may enlarge his interest to a freehold (s 153 of the LPA 1925).

Frustration

Frustration will rarely apply to a lease. However, it may be possible if the lease becomes incapable of performance for a significant proportion of the term (*National Carriers Ltd v Panalpina Ltd* (1981))

8 Mortgages

> A mortgage is a transaction under which land or chattels are given as security for the payment of a debt or the discharge of some other obligation.
>
> (*Santley v Wilde* (1899))

The owner of the land (the mortgagor) receives a loan in return for which he grants a mortgage to the mortgagee (nowadays usually a bank or building society). The agreement continues until the loan is repaid and the mortgage is redeemed.

Creation of legal mortgages

Freehold land

Two methods (s 85(1) of the LPA 1925):

- By demise.

- By legal charge.

Legal mortgages of registered land cannot be created by demise since 13 October 2003 (s 23(1) of the LRA 2002).

Freehold land by demise

Mortgagor grants a lease to the mortgagee subject to a provision for cesser on redemption. A first or only mortgagee takes a term for 3,000 years (s 85(2) of the LPA 1925).
Note: can now only be created if the land is unregistered.

Freehold land by legal charge

The mortgagee has the same protection, powers and remedies as if a mortgage of 3,000 years had been granted in his favour (s 87(1) of the LPA 1925).

Leasehold land

Two methods (s 86(1) of the LPA 1925):

- By sub-demise.

- By legal charge.

Legal mortgages of registered land cannot be created by sub-demise since 13 October 2003 (s 23(1) of the LRA 2002).

Leasehold land by sub-demise

Mortgagor grants a sublease to the mortgagee subject to a provision for cesser on redemption. A first or only mortgagee takes a term 10 days less than that of the mortgagor (s 86(2) of the LPA 1925).

Note: can now only be created if the land is unregistered.

The mortgagee has the same protection, powers and remedies as if a sub-term less by one day than the term vested in the mortgagor had been granted in his favour (s 87(1) of the LPA 1925).

Creation of equitable mortgages

- By valid contract under the rule in *Walsh v Lonsdale* (1882). The contract must be capable of specific performance and must comply with the relevant formalities (s 2 of the LP(MP)A 1989).

- By an express equitable charge.

- A mortgage of an equitable interest under a trust is always equitable. It must be in writing and signed by the mortgagor (s 53(1)(c) of the LPA 1925).

The method of creating a mortgage by deposit of title deeds or Land Certificate has not been possible since s 2 of the LP(MP)A 1989 came into force (*United Bank of Kuwait v Sahib* (1997)). After 26 September 1989, any attempt to create a mortgage by deposit alone will be ineffective and may lead to a successful negligence claim by the purported mortgagee (see *Dean v Allin & Watts* (2001) – solicitors liable after mortgage by deposit of title deeds was deemed void).

The mortgagor's equity of redemption

When the mortgagor grants a mortgage, he grants the mortgagee an interest in his land which is the equivalent of a legal estate (a term of years). The mortgagee therefore has a right to possession of the mortgaged property. The mortgagor is left with few legal rights to his property; but he does have his equity of redemption.

The equity of redemption is a collection of rights which may be summed up by the maxim 'once a mortgage always a mortgage' (*Seton v Slade* (1802)): the mortgagor must be free to redeem the mortgage at any time after the date set for redemption has passed (the date set for redemption is typically about six months after the creation of the mortgage). The equity of redemption comprises a number of rights, the most notable being the following:

- '*There should be no clogs or fetters on the equity of redemption*': the mortgagee must not attempt to exclude the right to redeem. Equity will not permit an option to purchase the mortgaged property in the mortgage deed, even if the option constitutes 'a perfectly fair bargain' (*Samuel v Jarrah Timber and Wood Paving Corp Ltd* (1904)). An option to purchase the mortgaged property may be valid if granted after the mortgage, however, because there is little likelihood of unconscionable conduct (*Reeve v Lisle* (1902)).

- '*There should be no unreasonable postponement of the right to redeem*': equity will prevent the mortgagee from gaining an unfair advantage (*Fairclough v Swan Brewery Co Ltd* (1912)). However, if the parties are two competent parties, acting under expert advice, and dealing at arm's length, the agreement will stand (*Knightsbridge Estates Trust Ltd v Byrne* (1940) – redemption not possible for 40 years).

- '*There should be no unfair collateral advantages*': a collateral advantage is an agreement contained in a mortgage or a

lease which does not relate to the mortgage or lease. The
collateral advantage often takes the form of a solus
agreement, whereby a mortgagor or lessee covenants only to
purchase supplies from the mortgagee or lessor. Such an
agreement will usually be enforceable only for the duration of
the mortgage (*Biggs v Hoddinott* (1898)) 'and necessarily
comes to an end upon payment off of the loan' (*Noakes and
Co Ltd v Rice* (1902)). If the mortgagor is able to prove that
the collateral advantage is fair and that it is not a clog on the
equity of redemption, it may be enforceable after the
mortgage has been redeemed (*Kreginger v New Patagonia
Meat and Cold Storage Co* (1914)). Solus agreements may
also be in restraint of trade and therefore contrary to Art 81
of the EEC Treaty.

● '*There should be no oppressive or unconscionable terms*':
the court may reduce a rate of interest which is deemed to
be unconscionable (*Cityland and Property (Holdings) Ltd v
Dabrah* (1968) – an annual rate of 19% reduced to 7%).
However, the test is unconscionability and harsh terms will
be allowed when businessmen are dealing 'at arm's length'
(*Multiservice Bookbinding Ltd v Marden* (1979)). If provided
for in the agreement, the mortgagee may alter interest rates,
provided that he does so in good faith, for valid commercial
reasons, and not for dishonest or improper purposes
(*Paragon Finance plc v Nash* (2001)). Mortgages may be
subject to ss 138 and 139 of the Consumer Credit Act 1972
and to the Unfair Terms in Consumer Contract Regulations
1999.

Undue influence and misrepresentation

Mortgagees themselves rarely exert undue influence or
misrepresent the terms of the mortgage. However, the
mortgagee may be unable to enforce the mortgage if it has
either actual or constructive notice of undue influence exerted
by a third party, or if the third party is deemed to have been

acting as the agent of the mortgagee (*Kings North Trust Ltd v Bell* (1986)).

Is the mortgagee tainted with undue influence exerted by a third party?

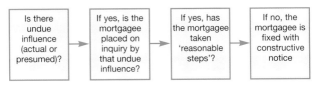

| Is there undue influence (actual or presumed)? | If yes, is the mortgagee placed on inquiry by that undue influence? | If yes, has the mortgagee taken 'reasonable steps'? | If no, the mortgagee is fixed with constructive notice |

- *Actual and presumed undue influence*: if the claimant is able to establish actual undue influence he does not have to prove that the transaction has been disadvantageous to him (*CIBC Mortgages plc v Pitt* (1994)). Undue influence may be presumed in two circumstances: when the relationship between the parties automatically gives rise to the presumption (solicitor/client; doctor/patient, etc – identified as type 2(A) in *Barclays Bank plc v O'Brien* (1994)); or when the *de facto* relationship between the parties was one of trust and confidence (husband/wife or parent/child may fall into this category – type 2(B)). In cases of presumed undue influence, the claimant must establish that the transaction was to his disadvantage (*Dunbar Bank plc v Nadeem* (1998)).

- *Placing the mortgagee on inquiry*: the mortgagee will be on inquiry if the nature of the transaction is such that there is a substantial risk of undue influence (*Barclays Bank plc v O'Brien* (1994) – a wife mortgaged her share in the matrimonial home to act as surety for her husband's business debts; she obtained no advantage from the transaction).

- *Taking reasonable steps*: the steps were enunciated by Lord Nicholls in *Royal Bank of Scotland plc v Etridge (No 2)* (2001):

- If the bank is not to provide face-to-face advice itself, the wife should be asked to choose a solicitor to advise her.
- The bank must provide the solicitor with details of the husband's financial circumstances.
- The bank may rely on the advice given by the solicitor unless it is aware of adverse circumstances that were not made known to the solicitor:
  - the solicitor must hold a face-to-face meeting without the husband;
  - he must explain to the wife: the effect of the transaction; the nature of the risk, considering the husband's financial circumstances; he must emphasise that the decision rests with the wife; and he must confirm that she wishes to proceed with the transaction.

- *The remedy*: if the bank is fixed with constructive notice of the undue influence or misrepresentation, the charge will be set aside in its entirety (*TSB Bank v Camfield* (1995)).

The remedies of the mortgagee

The right to sue on the covenant to repay

Section 20(1) of the LA 1980 sets a 12-year limitation period for recovery of the principal sum. The limitation period for the recovery of interest is six years (s 20(5)).

The power of sale

Available when the mortgage has been granted by deed – equitable mortgagees may apply under s 91(2) of the LPA 1925).

- The power must have arisen (s 101 of the LPA 1925) and have become exercisable (s 103).

- According to s 103 of the LPA 1925, the power of sale arises when: either the mortgagor has been in default for three months following the service upon him of a notice requiring payment of the mortgage money; or some interest on the mortgage has remained unpaid for two months after becoming due; or there has been a breach of some mortgage term other than a covenant to repay.

- When the property is sold the mortgagee holds the proceeds in trust (s 105).

- After costs have been met and mortgagees repaid in order of priority, any surplus is to be paid to the mortgagor (*Halifax Building Society v Thomas* (1996)).

- The mortgagee has a duty to obtain a true market value for the property, but not necessarily the best price possible (*Cuckmere Brick Co Ltd v Mutual Finance* (1971)).

The right to possession

- Available to legal mortgagees.

- The right to possession does not depend on the mortgagor's default – the mortgagor may go into possession 'before the ink is dry on the mortgage' (*Four-Maids Ltd v Dudley Marshall Ltd* (1957)).

- The court may grant relief to a mortgagor of a dwelling house if he is likely to be able to repay sums due under the mortgage within a reasonable period (s 36 of the AJA 1970).

- If the mortgagor intends to repay the mortgage by instalments, the starting point for determining a reasonable period is the remaining term of the mortgage (*Cheltenham and Gloucester BS v Norgan* (1996)), but a much shorter period of relief will be granted if the mortgagor intends to repay the mortgage by selling the property (*Target Home Loans Ltd v Clothier* (1994)).

- The time for determining whether or not a property is a dwelling is the time when proceedings are initiated (*Royal Bank of Scotland v Miller* (2001)).

- If the mortgagee sells the property without bringing an action or takes peaceable possession of the property whilst the mortgagor is not present at the property, the mortgagor may not claim relief under s 36 (*Ropaigealach v Barclays Bank plc* (1999)).

The right to appoint a receiver

- Available to a legal mortgagee (s 101(1) of the LPA 1925) – equitable mortgagees may apply under s 37(1) of the *Supreme Court Act 1981*).

- A receiver may be appointed if the power of sale has become exercisable (s 109 of the LPA 1925).

- A receiver owes a duty to the mortgagor to manage the property with due diligence (*Medforth v Blake* (1999)).

The right to foreclose

- When a mortgagee obtains an order for foreclosure the mortgagor's equity of redemption is extinguished and the property is in effect transferred to the mortgagee (ss 88 and 89 of the LPA 1925).

- Because it is such a draconian remedy, foreclosure is rarely granted, the court usually preferring to exercise its discretion under s 91(2) to award sale in lieu of foreclosure If the court decides to allow foreclosure, an order nisi will be granted, followed by an order absolute.

Protection of mortgages

- A legal mortgage of unregistered land, which is protected by deposit of title deeds, binds the world and does not require further protection. If it is not protected by deposit of title deeds it should be registered as a Class C(i) land charge in the Land Charges Register.

- An equitable mortgage of unregistered land should be protected by entry of either a Class C(iii) or a Class C(iv) land charge.

- A legal mortgage of registered land should be entered as a legal charge against the title to be charged.

- An equitable mortgage of registered land should be entered as a minor interest against the title to be charged.

9 Easements and profits *à prendre*

An easement is a right exercised over one plot of land (the servient tenement) for the benefit of another plot of land (the dominant tenement). We usually imagine an easement as a right of way or right to light, but there are many other rights that may be classified as easements, for example, a right to use a lavatory (*Miller v Emcer Products* (1956)) or a right to use neighbouring land as an airfield (*Dowty Boulton Paul Ltd v Wolverhampton Corp (No 2)* (1976)).

An easement must be distinguished from other similar rights:

- *Easements*: rights exercised for the benefit of one plot of land over another.

- *Profits à prendre*: rights to take something from land (eg, wood – a profit of estovers). The law regarding profits is similar to the law of easements.

- *Licences*: permissions to do something on the land. Licences are merely personal rights and are not interests in the land.

- *Customary rights*: rights in favour of the inhabitants of a particular community (*Mercer v Denne* (1905) – rights of members of a locality to dry fishing nets on the foreshore). Customary rights must be ancient, reasonable, certain and continuous (*Lockwood v Wood* (1844)). They are overriding interests for the purposes of registered land (para 4 of Sched 3 to the LRA 2002).

- *Public rights*: rights which are exercisable by any member of the public, such as public rights of way. Like easements, they may be acquired by prescription (long user), but they are not appurtenant to land. Public rights are overriding interests in registered land (para 5 of Sched 3 to the LRA 2002).

- *Natural rights*: natural rights are usually protected by the law of torts. They include a right of support for land (*Leakey v National Trust* (1980); *Holbeck Hall Hotel Ltd v Scarborough BC* (2000)).

Is the right claimed capable of being an easement?

The answer to this question is found in the four defining characteristics of an easement, as listed by Dankwerts J in *Re Ellenborough Park* (1956).

1 There must be dominant and servient tenement

An easement can only exist appurtenant to land. There must be two plots of land: one to take the benefit of the easement and another to take the burden. A profit, on the other hand, may exist 'in gross' – without a dominant tenement (*Bettison v Langton* (2002)).

2 The right claimed must accommodate the dominant tenement

The right must be of benefit to the dominant land and not just to a particular owner of it (*Hill v Tupper* (1863)). The two plots of land do not have to be contiguous (*Re Ellenborough Park* 1956)), but they must be close enough for the dominant tenement to obtain some benefit (*Bailey v Stephens* (1862)):

- The right must not be purely recreational (*Mouncey v Ismay* (1865)), but it is possible to acquire an easement to use a garden (*Re Ellenborough Park* (1956); *Mulvaney v Gough* (2002)).

3 The dominant and servient tenements must be owned by different persons

Obviously, you cannot have an easement over your own land (*Roe v Siddons* (1888)). However, if a landowner owns two plots of land and he exercises rights over one plot for the benefit of the other, such rights (known as quasi-easements) may become proper easements if one plot of land is sold (see *Wheeldon v Burrows* (1879) below). A tenant may acquire an easement over the land of his landlord.

4 The right claimed must be capable of forming the subject matter of a grant

- There must be a capable grantor and a capable grantee.

- The right must be sufficiently definite. There is no right to a view (*Aldred's Case* (1610)), or a right to light other than through a defined aperture.

- The right must be in the nature of rights traditionally categorised as easements, but 'the categories . . . must alter and expand with the changes that take place in the circumstances of mankind' (*Dyce v Lady James Hay* (1852)).

- The right must not amount to exclusive or joint user (*Copeland v Greenhalf* (1952); *Grigsby v Melville* (1974)).

- The right must not involve the servient owner in expenditure. An exception is easements of fencing (*Crow v Wood* (1971)).

The extent of some common easements

Rights of way

- The maintenance of the right of way is the responsibility of the grantee, unless there are circumstances to indicate the contrary (*Miller v Hancock* (1893)).

- The grantee may repair and improve the way if it was within the contemplation of the parties at the time of the grant (*Gerrard v Cooke* (1806)). If the right was acquired by prescription, the grantee may repair, but not improve, the way (*Mills v Silver* (1991)).

- Increased user will only be permitted if it was within the contemplation of the parties at the time of the grant (*Jelbert v Davis* (1968)). If the right was acquired by prescription, increased usage will be permitted provided that the nature of the user does not change (*British Railways Board v Glass* (1965); *Loder v Gaden* (1999)).

- A right of way acquired for the benefit of one plot of land may not be used to gain access to land adjoining the dominant tenement (*Harris v Flower* (1904); *Peacock v Custins* (2002); *Das v Linden Mews Ltd* (2002)).

Easements of light

- The right claimed must be a right to light through a defined aperture (eg, a window). In order to be actionable, interference with the right must affect the claimant's use and enjoyment of his land (*Colls v Home and Colonial Stores Ltd* (1904)).

- Even if the claimant succeeds in demonstrating that use of his building has been (or would be) affected, if the court decides that granting an injunction would be oppressive he may not be entitled to an injunction; he might have to rely upon damages in lieu (see *Midtown Ltd v City of London Real Property Co Ltd* (2005).

- Even a right to a high intensity of light may be acquired as an easement (*Allen v Greenwood* (1980) – right of light to a greenhouse).

Easements of car parking

- It is possible to acquire an easement to park a car, but not in a specific space. The right must not leave the servient owner without any reasonable use of any part of his land (*London & Blenheim Estates Ltd v Ladbroke Retail Parks Ltd* (1994); *Batchelor v Marlow* (2001))

Creating an easement

The requirements of *Re Ellenborough Park* (1956) merely help us to decide whether a right is capable of being an easement. In order for the right to be enforceable, it must have been validly created and, if the right is to bind third parties, it may need to be protected. Easements may be acquired by grant or by reservation.

Methods of creating easements by grant

Express grant

Formal grants must be by deed and they are usually incorporated into a conveyance or transfer of the legal estate. They must be 'for an interest equivalent to an estate in fee simple absolute in possession or a term of years absolute' to be legal (s 1(2)(a) of the LPA 1925).

Informal grant

Easements may be created by valid contract under the rule in *Walsh v Lonsdale* (1882). The grant relies on the remedy of specific performance and will be equitable only.

Estoppel

An easement may be acquired by estoppel (*ER Ives Ltd v High* (1967)).

Statute

Many easements were created long ago by the Inclosure Acts. More recently, easements have been created by statute in favour of public utilities (eg, for gas or electricity pylons, cables or pipes, etc). Such rights are often termed wayleaves.

- A statutory licence may be obtained by a landowner if he needs to enter onto neighbouring land in order to perform work which is reasonably necessary for the preservation of his land (Access to Neighbouring Land Act 1992). The order awarded by the court under this Act is similar to an easement, but the right of access terminates when the work has been completed.

Implied grant of necessity

A grant will only be implied out of necessity if it is impossible to enjoy land without such a grant (*Wong v Beaumont Property Trust Ltd* (1965)). The obvious example is when a plot of land would be landlocked without the implication of an easement.

Grant implied to give effect to the common intention of the parties

Nickerson v Barraclough (1981).

The rule in Wheeldon v Burrows (1879)

The rule implies an easement when a number of requirements are satisfied:

- *There must be unity of seisin before the grant*: when a landowner owns two adjacent plots of land and he exercises a quasi-easement over one plot for the benefit of another, the quasi-easement may become a proper easement if he sells the dominant land. Provided that:

  - the right is continuous and apparent at the time of the grant; and

  - the right is necessary for the reasonable enjoyment of the land (*Wheeler v JJ Saunders Ltd* (1995)).

Section 62 of the Law of Property Act 1925

Section 62 has been interpreted as being capable of turning a licence into an easement. As there has to be diversity of ownership before the grant, s 62 usually applies when a landlord renews a lease (*Wright v Macadam* (1949)) or when he sells the freehold to his tenant (*Hair v Gillman* (2000)). In order to avoid the consequences of s 62, a landlord may either revoke the licence before the conveyance or state a contrary intention in the conveyance (s 62(4)). There are two requirements:

- s 62 requires a conveyance;

- there must be diversity of ownership before the grant (*Sovmots Investments Ltd v S of S for the Environment* (1979) the opposite of *Wheeldon v Burrows*).

- the diversity of ownership requirement was considered to be unnecessary when the right claimed is continuous and apparent in *P&S Platt v Crouch* (2005).

Prescription (rights acquired by long user)

There are three different methods of acquiring easements by prescription:

- *Common law prescription*: the claimant has to establish use since 1189.

- *Lost modern grant*: if the claimant can prove 20 years' use, the law may presume a lost grant (*Dalton v Angus and Co* (1881)).

- *The Prescription Act 1832*: after 20 years, a claim to an easement cannot be defeated by evidence that it began after 1189; after 40 years the right becomes indefeasible unless the original use was as a result of consent or agreement (s 2); the periods for profits are 30 and 60 years (s 1); rights to light become indefeasible after 20 years (s 3). All periods must be 'next before some suit or action' (s 4).

Whatever method is relied upon, there are a number of requirements:

- The user must be the fee simple owner (*Simmonds v Dobson* (1991)).

- The user must be continuous (the right must not have been abandoned).

- The user must be as of right (*R v Oxfordshire CC ex p Sunningwell Parish Council* (2000)), which means user nec vi (without force), nec clam (without secrecy), and nec precario (it must not be exercised as a result of permission given by the servient owner).

Reservation of easements

Express reservation

In the event of doubt or ambivalence the terms will be construed against the party reserving the right.

Implied reservation of necessity

A reservation will only be implied if the land is landlocked or is incapable of use without the reservation (*Union Lighterage Co v London Graving Dock Co* (1902)). As a result, implied reservation is very rare – for a rare example, see *Sweet v Sommer* (2004).

Reservation implied to give effect to the common intention of the parties

A reservation will rarely be implied to give effect to the intention of the parties (*Re Webb's Lease* (1951); *Holaw (470) v Stockton Estates Ltd* (2000)). A notable exception is *Peckham v Ellison* (1998).

Protection of easements

Unregistered land

Legal easements and profits are rights *in rem* and bind the whole world.

Equitable easements created after 1925 are registrable as Class D(iii) land charges; if created before 1926 they are subject to the doctrine of notice.

Registered land

Most legal easements will be entered on the register against the title affected.

Those legal easements which are not on the register may override first registration (para 3 of Sched 1 to the LRA 2002). In order to override a registered disposition under para 3 of Sched 3, the easement must have been exercised within the past year or it must be within the actual knowledge of the purchaser, or the easement must have been discoverable by a reasonably careful inspection of the land.

Equitable easements should be entered as minor interests.

Reservation of easements

Easements

Alteration and extinguishment of easements

Alteration or realignment of an easement is rarely possible without the agreement of both parties (*B & Q plc v Liverpool and Lancashire Properties Ltd* (2001)), but in *Greenwich Health Care NHS Trust v London & Quadrant Housing Trust* (1998) realignment of a right of way was permitted because realignment was of considerable public benefit.

Easements do not lapse, but there are a number of ways by which they may come to an end:

- *Express release*: the dominant owner releases the servient owner from the obligation by deed.

- *Unity of possession and ownership*: you cannot have an easement over your own land.

- *Implied release*: there must be an intention on the part of the dominant owner to abandon the easement permanently. This may be difficult to prove – in *Benn v Hardinge* (1992), a non-user for 175 years was not sufficient for the implication of abandonment without evidence of an intention to abandon permanently (*Gotobed v Pridmore* (1970); *CDC2020 v Ferreira* (2005). The Law Commission (Report 254) recommended that there should be a rebuttable presumption of abandonment if the right has not been used for 20 years.

10 Freehold covenants

This chapter is concerned with freehold covenants, that is, covenants affecting freehold land.

A covenant is merely a promise or a contract. The word 'covenant' used to be used as a synonym for the word 'contract', but it is now usually used in a more technical sense to mean a 'promise', made by deed, to use land (or not to use land) in a certain way or for a certain purpose. Consider the following example:

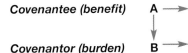

Covenantee (benefit)   A ——> X

Covenantor (burden)   B ——> Y

In the example, B has entered into a covenant with A. Let us imagine that the covenant is a promise that B will not use his property for business purposes. The person who makes the promise, in this case B, is known as the covenantor and the person to whom the promise is made, in this case A, is the covenantee. Because A and B are in privity of contract, A is able to enforce the promise against B.

In time, however, the land will be sold. If A sells his land to X, who was not a party to the original contract, X will want to enforce the covenant against B. In order to do so, X must establish that he has the benefit of the covenant. In order to do this, the benefit of the covenant must pass with the land (the term that we usually use is that the covenant must 'run with the land'). X is known as the assignee of the covenantee.

If B sells his land to Y (the assignee of the covenantor), it must be established that the burden of the covenant has run with the land to Y before he can be sued on the covenant. If both plots of land have been sold, X may want to sue Y, in which case both the benefit and the burden of the covenant must have run with the land. The rules for running covenants at law differ from the rules in equity.

The original parties

In the above example, A is able to enforce the covenant against B because they are in privity of contract. However, if B covenanted for the benefit B, his successors in title and 'the owners and occupiers of adjoining property', the owners of adjoining land, may take the benefit of the covenant because the covenant has been made for their benefit (s 56 of the LPA 1925; *White v Bijou Mansions* (1938); *Re Shaw's Application* (1995).

Contracts (Rights of Third Parties) Act 1999

C(ROTP)A 1999 provides that a person may enforce a contract 'in his own right' if the contract either provides that he may or if it 'purports to confer a benefit upon him'.

- C(ROTP)A applies only to contracts created after 11 May 2000.

- It provides that rights may be enforced by the third party provided that he is expressly identified in the contract by name or a 'a member of a class or as answering a particular description'.

- For the purposes of C(ROTP)A, persons described generically need not be in existence when the contract is entered into.

- There is no requirement that the covenant should 'touch and concern' the land, nor even that the third party seeking to enforce the covenant should be entitled to an estate in the land.

Running the benefit of covenants at law

There are four requirements:

- The covenant must 'touch and concern' the land. It must not be purely personal.

- The parties must have intended the benefit to run with the land. This will generally be presumed by virtue of s 78 of the LPA 1925.

- The covenantee must hold a legal estate in the land. The covenantor does not have to own any land (*The Prior's Case* (1368)).

- The assignee of the covenantee must also hold a legal estate in the land. It does not have to be the same legal estate (*Smith and Snipes Hall Farm v River Douglas Catchment Board* (1949)).

Running the benefit of a covenant in equity

There are three methods.

By assignment

The benefit of the covenant may be expressly assigned by the covenantee to his successor. There are three requirements (*Miles v Easter* (1933)): the covenant must have been taken for the protection or benefit of land owned by the covenantee at the date of the covenant; the assignment must be contemporaneous with the transfer of the dominant land; and the dominant tenement must be ascertainable.

By annexation

The annexation may be expressed or implied by virtue of s 78 of the LPA 1978 (*Federated Homes Ltd v Mill Lodge Properties Ltd* (1980)).

- The benefited land must be clearly identified (*Renals v Cowlishaw* (1978); *Crest Nicholson Residential Ltd v McAllister* (2004)).

By scheme of development (building scheme)

Schemes of development are usually created by a developer who obtains identical covenants from each purchaser of properties on the development. The covenants may then be enforced by any member of the development against any member who breaches the covenants. The original requirements were laid down in *Elliston v Reacher* (1908):

- Plaintiff and defendant must acquire title from a common vendor.

- The vendor must have laid out the scheme in lots.

- The covenants must have been intended to benefit all of the lots.

- Both purchaser and defendant must have purchased their properties with knowledge of the scheme and with an intention to be bound.

- The area affected by the scheme must be clearly defined (added by *Reid v Bickerstaff* (1909)).

The absence of the third requirement did not prevent the finding of a building scheme in *Baxter v Four Oaks Properties* (1965), and the absence of the first requirement was not fatal in *Re Dolphin's Conveyance* (1970). The more modern cases have tended to concentrate on the requirements 'reciprocity of obligation' and an intention to establish a system of 'local laws' (*Jamaica Life Assurance Society v Hillsborough Ltd* (1989)).

A landlord may also create a letting scheme whereby tenants may enforce obligations between themselves (*Williams v Kiley* (2002)).

Running the burden at law

The burden cannot run at common law because an obligation cannot be enforced against anybody who is not a party to the covenant (*Austerberry v Corp of Oldham* (1885)).

Running the burden in equity

The burden of a covenant may run in equity under the rule in *Tulk v Moxhay* (1848). In *Tulk*, it was decided that a purchaser of land from the covenantor is bound by the covenant if he purchased the land with notice of the covenant. For covenants created before 1926, the rule as to notice remains the same, but covenants created after 1925 must be registered in order to bind the assignee of the covenantor. If title to the land is registered, the covenant should be entered as a notice at the Land Registry; if the land is unregistered it should be entered as a Class D(ii) land charge in the Land Charges Register.

There are also four further conditions precedent before the burden will run (*Haywood v Brunswick Permanent Benefit Building Society* (1881)) under the rule in *Tulk v Moxhay*:

- *The covenant must be negative or restrictive in nature*: the burden of a positive covenant cannot run. A positive covenant requires expenditure of money or labour: for example, a covenant to keep a property in good repair is positive. The test is one of substance – it does not matter how the covenant is worded, so a covenant not to permit a property to fall into disrepair is also positive.

- *The covenantee must at the time the covenant is made and afterwards own the land which benefits from the covenant* (*London CC v Allen* (1914)).

- *The covenant must touch and concern the dominant land*.

- It must be the common intention of the parties that the burden of the covenant shall run with the land of the covenantor: this will usually be implied, unless a contrary intention is expressed, by virtue of s 79 of the LPA 1925.

The problem of positive covenants

Because of the rules in *Austerberry* and *Tulk v Moxhay* (1848), the burden of a positive covenant cannot run with freehold land.

Some properties, however, require enforceable positive obligations for the management and maintenance of the land. For example, the occupiers of a block of flats need to ensure that the common parts (landings, stairways, lifts, etc) are maintained. For this reason, most flats have tended to be leasehold, so that a covenant to maintain the common parts can be enforced as a leasehold covenant.

A number of methods of enforcing positive covenants with freehold land have been tried with varying degrees of success:

- Identical covenants may be taken by each successive purchaser, thereby forming a chain of indemnity. The chain can be broken, however.

- The doctrine of mutual benefit and burden may apply (*Halsall v Brizell* (1957)). The benefit must be related to the burden (*Rhone v Stephens* (1994)) and the burden will only be enforced if the assignee chooses to exercise the benefit (*Thamesmead Town Ltd v Allotey* (1998)).

- Section 79 of the LPA 1925 is unlikely to be useful, as it does not annex the burden of a covenant to the land (*Tophams v Earl of Sefton* (1967); *Rhone v Stephens* (1994)).

- A long lease may be granted, which is then enlarged to a fee simple (s 153(1) of the LPA 1925).

- An estate rentcharge may be created for the maintenance of the property (s 2(3)(c) of the Rentcharges Act 1977).

- A right of entry may be reserved (*Shiloh Spinners Ltd v Harding* (1973)).

- Tenants of flats may form a management company to be the landlord. The company is then able to enforce positive obligations under the lease.

- New developments may be subject to the Commonhold and Leasehold Reform Act 2002. In a commonhold scheme, the landowners (unit holders) hold a freehold estate in commonhold land. This is a freehold together with an

The problem of positive covenants

Freehold covenants

unseverable share in a commonhold association (a company formed to own the common parts and manage the commonhold land). The commonhold association is able to enforce positive obligations against the unit holders. Existing developments may be converted to a commonhold scheme, but only if all parties agree to the change.

Discharge and modification of covenants

- *By unity of seisin*: if both plots of land come into common ownership, the covenant cannot be enforced.

- *By release*: the covenantee may release the covenantor by deed, or release may be implied from the facts. For example, if the character of the neighbourhood has changed so as to make the covenant worthless, or if the covenantee has acquiesced in open breaches, it may be held that the covenantee has impliedly released the covenantor from the obligation, or that he has abandoned the covenant.

- *By the Lands Tribunal*: s 84(1) of the LPA 1925 gives the Lands Tribunal powers to modify or discharge covenants in such circumstances as obsolescence.

Remedies for breach of covenant

- *Common law damages*: available when the original covenantee sues the original covenantor or when the assignee of the covenantee sues the original covenantor (*Surrey CC v Bredero Homes Ltd* (1993)).

- *Interlocutory injunction*.

- *Final injunction*.

- *Equitable damages – damages in lieu of an injunction under s 50 of the* Supreme Court Act 1981: for example, in *Wrotham Park Estate Ltd v Parkside Homes Ltd* (1974), damages in lieu of an injunction were awarded because to order demolition of a housing estate, which had been built in breach of covenant, would be a waste of good housing.